DEBACLE
TO
DELIGHT

THE BLESSING *of* GRACE
THROUGH ADVERSITY

CHRIS ROCHE

Debacle to Delight

The blessing of Grace through adversity

Chris Roche

ISBN (Print Edition): 978-1-54398-841-3

ISBN (eBook Edition): 978-1-54398-842-0

TABLE OF CONTENTS

For this cause I bow my knees unto the Father of our Lord Jesus Christ

Of whom the whole family in heaven and earth is named,

That He would grant you, according to the riches of His glory, to be strengthened with might by His Spirit in the inner man,

That Christ may dwell in your hearts by faith; that ye, being rooted and grounded in love,

May be able to comprehend with all saints what is the breadth, and length, and depth, and height;

And to know the love of Christ which passeth knowledge, that ye might be filled with all the fullness of God.

Now unto Him that is able to do exceedingly abundantly above all that we ask or think, according to the power that worketh in us,

Unto Him be glory in the church by Christ Jesus throughout all ages, world without end. Amen.

— EPHESIANS 3:14-21

Once in Bondage but now set free
An incredible miracle happened to me
A complete emotional wreck I was then
Discouraged and depressed faith so thin
Carrying heavy baggage for 30 years
Even as an adult breaking out in tears
For pain and suffering that I caused
There were moments of fear all was lost
But the Redeemer had a heavenly plan
To restore and reconcile this sinful man
Addiction of control brought anxiety so high
My life was uncontrollable I cannot deny
Into the darkest depths of despair I went
With confusion and torment my mind was bent
Cycles of fear and anger certainly a sin
Looking to others for worth an idol within
It was only for Him to breathe life in me
Seeking satisfaction elsewhere an errant plea
Uncertainty would always come through the door
Who would Chris be today, the stress was a chore
From spiritual desert bones so dry
The more I failed, the harder I would try
Only God can help you she would say to me
But I was not advancing so she had to flee
What courage and faithfulness it took
It was a wakeup call to make me look
The course of action was radically drastic
However, the end result was utterly fantastic
Such crushing pain there was no lack

But Jesus knew it would bring me back
At the bottom on my face was my condition
Broken looking to Him my new position
My performance was never up to task
What liberation when finally taking off the mask
The word was out, my sin exposed
No sense in hiding, everybody knows
Time alone with God is what I needed
The council of His word I heeded
God knew I needed temporary isolation
In that quiet place, there was consecration
Seeking forgiveness, I was found kneeling
Guilt and condemnation no more, but healing
Truly repentant of choices in my soul
Looking to Jesus only to make me whole
Although many regrets and much time lost
Jesus has forgiven at a precious cost
Opportunity gone by, feeling deep sorrow
The Lord forgives and brings a new tomorrow
The pain of the past went for so long
But now I gloriously sing a new song
Because of issues, I was rightly faulted
Now through magnificent Grace, Christ is exalted
Devastating debacle to Divine delight
Fear no longer overcomes to indict
What liberty did confession bring to light
Through it all relationships were made right
Psalm 51 has been my daily devotion
Bringing about changes set into motion

From fleshly effort and working I cease

With a loving yoke, God guides with ease

Abiding in His presence is now my desire

Righteous by faith from this purifying fire

Now complete and secure in Christ alone

No more fear and anxiety in my home

Many years to get past hurt feelings

This servant now knows true healing

I know my sin well and others do too

Salvation is now my joy through and through

No longer are there sins to hide

Once dry bones have come alive inside

No longer in bondage to my past

True freedom in Christ that will last

Transformation of this man by God's power

Taking steadfast refuge in his strong tower

Jesus you have cracked the crusty shell

Saturate me with the living water well

To a place of prayer I have never known

The depths of Christ love I wholeheartedly own

To laugh, love, and live is my desire

With Christ at the center bringing me higher

Fully entrusted to His Grace now

With the armor of God, set to the plow

In an engulfing love there is no strife

Ministry to others will now be my life

An incredible thing happened to me

Lord, use this story to set captives free

INTRODUCTION

I **HAVE TRIED TO SIT DOWN AND WRITE THIS STORY FOR** several years, but until now, have not been successful in doing so. Maybe because of laziness, maybe because of procrastination, or maybe some lack of inspiration. But now I sit down to write again and attempt to tell a story that is very dear to me. A story about how God used a traumatic situation to get my attention. The truth is that some of the elements of the poem in the previous pages, now used as a framework for this book, had not come to reality yet. Having had written the poem several years ago, there were still parts that had not been fulfilled in my life. The lessons learned have come at a great cost to myself and others. Some people learn lessons easy, but I seem to learn them very hard. But in the end, the result was good. I have told people that I am ashamed of things in my past, but am not embarrassed to talk about them. It is a great thing when we can open up and share our issues, our shortcomings, and our weaknesses. By doing so, we humble ourselves before God and before our fellow man in a way that brings encouragement, hope, and healing. As a matter of fact, it helps me to tell this story. To share my testimony is therapeutic and helps me to keep a proper perspective on life. I hope that by sharing these very intimate things, others' lives might be touched. Taking each day, one at a time, I found God faithful to carry me through.

On Monday, August 21, 2017, I was a witness to the total solar eclipse in North America. I wrote the following in my journal: This is the day when everything comes into alignment. The total solar eclipse will start at approximately 1:17 this afternoon. What a fantastic thing it is today when we get to see another example of God's majesty. His Sun, Moon, and Earth will come into alignment in a unique way. I am thankful to get to see this. As I sit writing this, it is 10:04 AM. I am sitting on a hill in Jefferson Barracks Park in St. Louis, overlooking the Mississippi River. Water flows down the river as people relax under shade trees and the birds sing. One can forget all the calamity in the world in a moment like this. Lord, may this be a time of focus and renewal. While the magnitude of what we are about to experience is significant, it is just a glimpse of the magnitude that awaits us in eternal heaven with you. Visible images that the human mind cannot even imagine.

"But it is written, eye hath not seen, nor ear heard, neither have entered into the heart of man, the things which God hath prepared for them that love him." I Corinthians 2:9

The eclipse that day did not disappoint. God's wonder and majesty never does. Everything came into alignment that day. When our lives come into alignment with God's eternal plan, the sensation can be overwhelming. I had been lost for so long, but now was found. When I came into alignment with Jesus, I began to have this insatiable desire to explore, to run, and to enjoy every aspect of life. In the past, I never really thought that much about flowers or taking walks in the park, but now, those things are special to me. Why? Because I can see God's hand in everything, as if the world opened-up to me. Some in the world say that a mind opened to the things of Christ makes them close-minded. But I beg to differ. A mind open to the things of Christ allows one to see, experience, and enjoy all the creation of God in a way not otherwise possible. There are a lot of people in the world doing things badly. I was one of those people. And even now, I know I'm not close to perfection, but I am close to the One who is perfect.

This path that I am on has been an astonishing path to take. I have met many interesting people and traveled to many distant places, but most of all, I have experienced an inner peace that I had never felt before. For those that are going through difficult times right now, I can only hope to encourage you to continue walking it out each day, trusting in the Lord God. When I talk to people about the process I've been through, I get really excited! Why do I get excited about this? Because I know what I know to be absolutely true. There is no coincidence and there are no accidents in this entire set of life circumstances, because God has had His hand on me the entire time. And it was a process to bring me back to him, into proper alignment with His life in me. I pray as you read through these following chapters, you would ask God to touch your heart in a meaningful way. And if you are experiencing a time of wilderness in your life, that you would open your heart to the grace, hope, and purpose He has for you.

Over the course of these chapters, I will be writing a lot of things about the negatives in my past life. Not so much to focus on being negative, but it is important to show the contrast. To share the depths of my soul and to open myself in confession is necessary to tell the story. Because there is always an opposite. Why does there have to be an opposite?

In Isaiah 45:7, the Bible states that God makes peace and creates evil. In the passage of I Kings 22:19-23, we read that God sent a lying spirit into the prophets of Ahab. In the book of Genesis, we read that Adam and Eve ate from the tree of the knowledge of good and evil. These are fascinating passages and while one thinks about them, the question could arise, "Where did the ability, in and of itself, come from for Lucifer to make the decisions he did?" I would suggest that God had to have created an opposite. Inherent in the Creation, there must have been the ability to take on selfishness, consequently resulting in rebellion. There had to be an opposite. Without evil, we would have no way of knowing what is good. Satan cannot create, he can only imitate. We might say that Satan is simply God's convenient agent. Would it be possible for us to know good today if we didn't know what evil (bad) was? I don't think so.

What tree did Adam and Eve eat from anyway? It was the tree of the knowledge of good and evil. It was not just of good and evil, but of the knowledge of what it meant. Certainly, I believe it was a physical tree with physical fruit, but with that also came a spiritual fruit. It was a spiritual event that opened their eyes and mind to the reality of the opposite. Thus set in guilt and shame and the imminent absence of God's Holiness. Not only until they acknowledged their wrong-doing and were rendered a punishment would God put them under His covering again. I just suspect this covering was most likely a coat from a slain lamb – a foreshadowing of the shedding of the Lamb's blood (Jesus Christ) for all mankind. When the eyes of both of them had been opened, they initially tried to cover themselves (works), but it was only the Lord that could properly cover them (grace). What opposite or contrast has the Lord put in your life today? The Lord desires that it will drive you closer to Him.

Is it possible that Adam and Eve were not fully aware of the greatness of God and the intimate and privileged preciousness of being in His presence until they were knowledgeable of the opposite (evil)? All of this is not to say that we enjoy evil or relish in its existence. It is simply to acknowledge it is real and has a purpose. Why? To show that God is good. So in writing this, I hope the "opposites" in my life would stand as a testimony of God's goodness. In my opinion, I think we are all contradictions in some way. But it is my prayer, that those redeemed contradictions, will eventually point others to Jesus. When Jesus takes that opposite, He can make a testimony.

CHAPTER 1:

THE TREASURE PATH

Once in Bondage but now set free
An incredible miracle happened to me

I SUPPOSE ONE DOESN'T KNOW HOW GOOD FREEDOM FEELS
unless they have been in some sort of bondage or prison. My life
was once filled with so much anxiety and fear that it was indeed a
prison. But something happened and everything changed. It was
the hand of God that put me on a path of healing. I believe it is
incredible because I am alive today to write about it. A good story
is worth telling. And for me, this is a good story. A story of how
God set me on a good path. A path that would lead me to tell this,
and in doing so, find peace and help others.

THE PATH I WAS ON

I believe it is inherent in our makeup to want to be at peace and
to be content. Eric Liddell, a Scottish missionary to China and an

Olympic runner, said, "*I believe God made me for a purpose, but he also made me fast! And when I run, I feel his pleasure.*" Liddell knew when he was operating in his gifting, He experienced God in a special way. But when we are trying to operate outside of God's plan, we struggle. This seems to be the reason so many people, including myself, continually find themselves struggling to find a place of rest. We want to be content. We want to be happy. But how is the question. Men have theorized and sought philosophy over the years, trying to find the key to happiness and contentment. The Scripture talks about people running to and fro following every wind of doctrine. Why is this? When that goal of peace and contentment is void of God, we consistently find ourselves in a state of disappointment and disillusionment. I would like to think the treasure path is that path in life God has each of us on, to draw us closer to him. Whether we realize it or not, He wants to draw us out of our current situation and into an intimate relationship. When He brings us into that special place, each person shall know what true peace and rest is. The path is the process of life that leads us to Him, the Treasure. The peace, contentment, and joy are the natural consequences of that relationship with Him. And nowhere else can we find it. But we struggle on in some vain effort to create systems and lifestyles, thinking we can go around the Answer to other more selfish manmade ideas. At least I did. It wasn't working.

COULD I GET THERE?

I always struggled to get to a place of rest. A counselor named Randy once talked to me about the difference between human-being and human-doing. The human-doing continually finds himself in a state of anxiety and unrest while the human-being has the ability to rest in the One who created Him. I am thankful for the counsel and ministry Randy sowed into my life. A pastor friend of mine would often tell stories of his early Christian walk. He and his wife, and some other friends traveled to many parts of the country looking for answers to their lives. They thought the next best seminar or convention might have the answer. Or maybe some cutting edge ministry with all types of fantastic programs. But in the end, he discovered a quiet place with God. After searching for many years, he found the treasure in the presence of God. It was during those last years of his life that I believe he was the most content. For me, I struggled for over thirty years with a lot of emotional issues. It can be painful to discover what our flaws are, and maybe even more painful to have them repaired. However, once healed, we experience a flow of life through of us that we could not have imagined before. For this, I am thankful. On April 24, 2018, I was riding a camel around the Great Pyramids in Egypt and had an overwhelming sense of peace and freedom that I had never experienced before. As I took that ride, I replayed a lot of events in my life. It took many years to get there, and over these next chapters, I will tell much of that story.

WHAT DOES GOD WANT FOR ME?

There is no doubt in my mind that God always wanted me to experience His peace. But I struggled to get there by wondering what my purpose was and found myself fighting a lot of insecurities. I seemed to be good at putting on a happy face to most people, but inside I was really hurting. The never-ending question in my mind was what should I be doing with my life. Why could I not feel settled? Why could I not experience the peace and rest I knew God wanted for me. The peace and rest that Jesus had secured for me. Ultimately, the answer is always this: God wanted me to be intentional in my walk by going to Him each day in prayer, seeking direction, and meditating on His Word. George Muller, a great minister to orphans in England, said, "*Thus, through prayer to God, the study of the Word, and reflections, I come to a deliberate judgement according to the best of my ability and knowledge, and if my mind is thus at peace, and continues to be after two or three more petitions, I proceed accordingly.*" I love this quote from Muller because it brings me back to proper perspective. With so many messages being pushed into our world, our only sure footing can be found in His Word. Not that we look for quick recipes, but this process that Muller went through for most of his life, is really the only answer we have. I don't know about you, but I can be stubborn and hard-headed. I wanted another way, but could not find it.

THERE WERE A LOT OF GOOD MOMENTS

When I would look around the house at the photos on the wall or flip through photo albums, people are always found smiling and having a good time in the pictures. It is interesting how we always choose the good photos to display, but rarely do you find a photo showing difficulty or struggle. There were a lot of good moments in my past life. I suppose the hundreds of photos showing smiling people is proof of that. But again, at a heart level, I was never content with my walk with the Lord and could not find rest. Oh Lord, the rest that I desired was seemingly so difficult to achieve. I would wonder about the passage of Scripture where Jesus tells us our burdens are light. Why could I not get there? I was simply trying to run on my own strength. I have spent a lot of time running. From running track in high school and college to running marathons, I have run a lot of miles. There is something called a runner's high. It is a wonderful sensation you get when you break through the pain and feel an elation unknown to the casual runner. You reach a point where you feel you cannot go on. But then you push yourself further. There is a point at which, you break through the pain and the body does an amazing thing. An energy shoots through the body, making you feel as if you could run forever. Unfortunately, in our flesh, this does not last long. When we run in our flesh, we can only sustain this energy for so long, until we die out. We get frustrated, we get tired, we get depressed, we get lonely, we get sad … the list goes on and on. But when we run in God's strength, it is as if we have the runner's high. Like Eric Liddell, we certainly do feel God's pleasure when we are doing what we were made to do.

GOING FROM A TO B IS NOT ALWAYS PRETTY

Do you believe God wants the best for you? Do you believe that God, through His Son Jesus Christ, is more than enough for you? I do. Sometimes that faith is tested. Sometimes that faith is tried in a way we cannot comprehend. A good friend of mine sometimes jokingly says, "*This is not what I signed up for.*" Sometimes he also refers to the rat race we find ourselves in … and the rats seems to be winning. Life is full of challenges and struggles. Some may have it easy, but I would guess that most of us could not say that. Everything is relative to what one may have lived or experienced, but we have struggles. And sometimes those struggles seem like a wilderness we cannot get out of. Michael Card writes, "*If, as you are reading this, you find yourself in the wilderness, realize that though you may not feel like it at the moment, you are in the very place where the Bible reveals that true worship can begin.*" What Card is saying is really good news. When I realized that this wilderness was a good place for me, joy began to take over the sadness. Why? Because I knew I was in a place where God could heal me. A place where He had brought me. A place of healing and worship. The easy path would not have brought me to this place. This place of precious holiness and intimacy with Christ. Having experienced this Holy of Holies place, in the prayerful mind, I began to realize that my treasure path was taking turns toward His purpose. I love the fact that as I write these words, I am reminded of His Grace. It is by His Grace that I sit and write this testimony. It is by His Grace that I can mindfully write out these memories and lessons. I pray God will use them to help someone. For me, going from A to B in life has been a rough road. But now I look back and see intention, hope, and purpose in life. That someone might come to know God better by reading these words … what more meaningful purpose could I have? I cannot think of anything more important.

God's Path of Grace

Do you really believe there is a God? I certainly do. And if so, do you really believe that He loves you? It is my opinion that many people believe God is loving, but we might question how His love should be expressed. One can easily have some misunderstanding about love. I do not claim to have all the answers, but I do know this. God's love includes sadness, discipline, and judgement. Just as a parent must sometimes take drastic measures to get their child's attention, God must do the same with us. It is His nature to do so. It is who He is. To let us go on in our misguided sinful life would go against everything that He is. In writing about the story of Job, Michael Card also writes, "*So He allows a painful mystery to begin. "He is in your hands." the father sighs. And Job's ordeal, and our, begins.*" An ordeal. Being alone. Having my family torn apart. Staring at the prospect of a divorce. For me, it was an ordeal I never imagined could have happened. I use the phrase 'by His Grace' a lot in this book. This is because the grace of God was the pivotal and determining factor in my life and death situation. When we view sin as it should be, we realize that life and death really is at stake. The idea that God could take me, by the Grace of Jesus Christ, into a new life of purpose, is Grace. Grace and Hope just go together. They are inseparable, and when the plan of God comes together in my life and yours, there is a celebration in heaven. Only by His Grace can we get back on the path of purpose and hope. I am so thankful for this!

WHAT WE VALUE

What is valuable to you? Life is valuable and most precious. On a flight from Dallas to Tokyo, I sat about ten feet across the aisle from a man that was going into diabetic shock. The man's wife was sitting in the row behind him and she immediately jumped over the seats and straddled his body. She started slapping his face screaming, "Breathe, breathe, breathe!!" The attendants on the plane quickly came over the intercom requesting anyone with medical training to help. It was a very traumatic moment. There were two young nurses on the plane that seemed to be in their early twenties. They came back and jumped to the task with eagerness and willingness. It was about this same time that the flight attendants were coming through the cabin passing out everyone's dinner. I sat there and stared at the food on my tray with my arms crossed and thought there was no way I could eat while a man across the aisle could die. I was shocked and amazed to look around and see people eating their food and watching a movie as if nothing was happening. Again, I looked at the man's wife desperately trying to help revive her husband. My heart was breaking for her and then I started to pray. Eventually the nurses were able to get his blood sugar to level out and he recovered. What a fantastic event. I sat there with tears streaming down my face thankful for those young ladies that had jumped to the occasion and literally saved his life. Many people in life today are casually eating and entertaining themselves while people next to them are dying. When we are on this path that God has put us on, we never know what can happen or what will result as our consequences unfold. It is during times like this we should be thankful for life and thankful for the breath He gives each day. Just like that eclipse, it was spectacular. When I started to come into alignment with God and His Word, my life began to have a meaning and purpose I had not experienced before.

MOMENTS IN LIFE

When I started seeking the real Treasure of Christ, priorities changed, and I started finding significance. On April 24, 2018, I was sitting inside the King's Chamber in the Great Pyramid

Khufu. This was my second trip to Egypt and as I sat alone in that room, I thanked God for what He had done in my life. The evening before, I was talking to one of the local Egyptian guides I had become friends with. I asked Mohammed if there was any way that I could enter the Pyramid early the next morning before it was open to the public. He told me to meet him at 7:15 the next morning. The window from my room at the Guardian Guest House, directly across from the Giza Plateau, offered a tremendous view of the Pyramid even as I laid my head on my pillow. I laid in bed that night, thankful for being there. The next morning, he was there at our meeting place as planned and we proceeded up the hill, past the Sphinx, and then on to meet with a guard-friend of his at the site. The guard was kind enough to let me in. I told them I wanted about thirty minutes inside by myself and they said no problem. It was quite an amazing feeling to be by myself inside that magnificent structure. I made my way through the winding passages, then up the grand gallery, and eventually lowered myself to enter the King's Chamber. There is something quite unique about being in the King's Chamber. It is a quiet place. It is a place of absolute solitude. It is a place of silence. And for me that day, it was a place of peace.

Inside is a sarcophagus that never held a body. When the chamber was discovered it was empty. An empty tomb. I sat on the floor with my journal for about fifteen minutes and then walked around the perimeter of the room touching each stone I could reach. As I touched each stone, I prayed to God. I thanked Him for His goodness, and then asked Him for a future filled with things that only He could do. I pulled a piece of legal paper out of my shirt pocket and wrote the following words, *"Thank you Lord Jesus for this time in Egypt. It has been three years today and now I sit alone in the King's Chamber and thank you for all that has happened to me. You know my future and I will trust you!"* Three years after my radical process had begun, I would be enjoying this special moment in Egypt. The three years in between had been quite difficult and sometimes felt impossible. But now I felt more liberty than I had my entire life. That slip of legal paper is now tucked away in the pages of my Bible.

WHAT I WANTED TO BE AND WHAT I ACTUALLY LIVED

Some of our problems are self-inflicted, while some are due to external forces, and out of our control. But I sincerely believe God uses every situation to bring us to a crossroad. What direction will we take? Will we continue down the path of self, that destructive path of self-preservation? Or while at the crossroad, will we choose to turn toward the will of God? That perfect path paved by God to bring us into closer relationship with Him. Yes, the mystery may be painful, but what glorious results it can bring if yielded to it. The Lord wants us engaged in quiet time with Him. To get alone with God. To find the Holy of Holies in our heart by allowing His Word to penetrate every aspect of our life. Hudson Taylor wrote, *"Our attention is here drawn to a danger, which is pre-eminently one of this day; the intense activity of our times may lead to zeal in service, to the neglect of the personal communion; but such neglect will not only lessen the value of the service, but tend to incapacitate us for the highest service."* What Hudson Taylor is saying here is quite profound but at the same time so simple. I was guilty of this myself. Forsaking that precious communion with my Lord and Savior Jesus. Instead,

I would always find myself running here and there trying to accomplish this or that. The zeal for service or other physical activities of busyness often get in the way. When God sets us on this treasure path to know Him for who He truly is, He also sets into motion ways and methods necessary to get us to His desired outcome.

IT IS TRULY AN EXCITING NEW LIFE

A life with God will bring about a new outlook. That which was once dead comes alive. And that which was dark, it now bright with the light of hope in our Creator. Seeing life through a new set of lenses will cause us not only to appreciate the magnitude of His creation, but will also give us a deep appreciation and care for other people. There is an African proverb that says, *"Do not laugh at seeing a boat tossed in the sea, because your brother might be in it."* How true this is! We never know what people are going through and it may be someone that needs our help. And on other occasions, we may find ourselves in that boat being tossed by the wind. This idea of caring for one another is really one of humility and when we have humility in our lives, God can work in and through us. But the prideful person will never experience this part of the path God wants them on. Oh, that each of us might humble ourselves before God. It is so important. Our life is a gift. It is a gift from a Heavenly Father that will love us unconditionally and without fail. He loves us in our sin, but loves us too much to leave us in that condition. I am so thankful He saved me. And the truth bears witness He is continually saving me each day. In the book of James, we find a passage that speaks to proper perspective. We read in James 4:14, *"whereas you do not know what will happen tomorrow. For what is your life? It is even a vapor that appears for a little time and then vanishes away."* James reminds us here of the limited time we have, and when we see the significance of it, we should begin to live each day the way our Creator intended. To be in fellowship and worship with Him in all that we do.

CHAPTER 2:

IN BONDAGE

A complete emotional wreck I was then
Discouraged and depressed faith so thin
Carrying heavy baggage for 30 years
Even as an adult breaking out in tears

SEVERAL YEARS PRIOR TO WRITING THIS, I WAS GOING
through such internal turmoil that I could barely function. It is a
real shame that I didn't seek help for my problems earlier in life. I
kept thinking things would get better with time. But by the time
changes did occur, some 30 years had past. During that time, I
was in a continual loop of discouragement and, I probably didn't
realize it, depression. I was experiencing an all-out spiritual battle
for my soul and discouragement was winning the day. The sadness
caused by my many ups-and-downs would cause me to break out
in tears … just wanting to feel some relief.

What was my problem?

There was really a void in my heart. Even though I was a Christian, I was not truly believing and trusting in God. I had accepted the work of Christ in my life at the age of 9. I can remember walking to a friend's house after school for a Bible study. His family hosted an after-school study at their house once a week. It was at one of these meetings, that for the first time, I felt the call of God on my life. So at the age of 9, after hearing the gospel message, I decided to give my life to Jesus. But it wasn't until many years later that I would actually commit my life to serving him with my whole self. Until recently, my relationship with the Lord seemed to be one of convenience. When I was down and needed something, I would pray. Or maybe someone had a health issue so I would pray. It was really a selfish way to worship. Honestly, it probably wasn't worship at all. Rather, I was still living for Chris and wanting things my way. Ultimately, I had a sin problem. Michael Reeves writes, "*For in the Bible, sin is something that goes deeper than our behavior. Indeed, we can do what is "right" and be no better than whitewashed tombs, clean on the outside but rotten on the inside. Jonathan Edwards argued that even the demons can do what is 'right' in that superficial sense of good behavior.*" It seems I was always hoping who I was, instead of truly examining who I really was. Being in bondage is a terrible thing. Like a prison that chained me to a problem, I could not find freedom. I had a lot of mood swings. Maybe it was pride and arrogance. Maybe it was fear. When people would ask me how I was doing, I would often respond, "I am doing great!" But inside that really wasn't the case. It is a shame that when asked that question, so many people deny the opportunity to get honest with people and share their needs. More often than not, that was the case with me. The cycle of fear, control, and anger was dominating my life. It was terrible for me and those around me.

I always thought I had things figured out. It is incredible to think that I actually used to look down on people with problems, when I had so many of my own. I am so thankful my thinking has changed. Now I have compassion on people's problems, because I have learned from my own.

THE DEVIL MADE ME DO IT?

Many people want to blame others for their problems or short-comings. A frequent target of blame is the devil himself. Certainly, the devil is described as an enemy in the Bible. The Bible also says this enemy is roaming about seeking whomever he can devour. So this is not something we should take lightly. While some want to blame the devil for everything, some don't believe in him at all. In writing about her great missionary work in Northern Thailand, Isobel Kuhn wrote, "*The only person who does not believe that the Devil is a person is someone who has never attempted to combat him or his ways ... the simple tribesman going through his animistic incantations is wiser than such a drugged intellectual. He, at least, knows there is a Devil; and he has ways to appease him temporarily.*" Kuhn certainly knew what she was talking about. Having experienced many ups-and-downs on the missionary field, she realized the reality of the spiritual battle that is being waged every day. And while it is true that the enemy is a destructive foe, it is also true that he cannot make us do anything. The Word of God makes it clear he can tempt us. He can lie to us. He can try to deceive us.

But ultimately, he cannot make us do anything. For the believer in Christ, one can simply cast every thought and every imagination on to Jesus. Jesus has already fought and won every battle that we will face. We simply have to acknowledge that and rest in Him. But for me, in my old condition, I was not doing that. I was still caught up in my bondage and was yet to put my full trust in God.

I WAS SO ANGRY

Anger is powerful and destructive. When I think about anger, I can recall an evening in Mumbai, India. I had been invited to a friend's house for a visit. Madhavi, one of the trustees of the orphanage we did adoption work through, gave me a tour of her house. After we visited and talked about the orphanage, she called a cab for my ride back to the hotel. Her home was about 45 minutes from the city-center where I was staying at the Sheraton. The cab arrived at her house, and after our goodbyes, I set off for the city. About twenty minutes into my trip, the driver began to curse the American government for the ongoing war in Iraq. I listened to his tirade for what seemed to be over ten minutes. The anger that was coming out of his mouth was quite frightening. This was one of the few times in all my travels that I got a bit nervous. The other was getting lost near a slum outside of Nairobi, Kenya, but that story is for a different time. After he calmed down a bit, I thanked him for the ride and told him how much I had been enjoying my stay in India. He seemed to be satisfied with that and gladly took my money for the ride. Anger. It is a powerful thing. It can control the person with the problem and also hold others in fear around them.

The cycle of fear, control, and anger is a vicious cycle. For over 30 years, I was found caught in this deadly cycle. It was deadly spiritually and deadly emotionally. What a terrible place to be in. I would often find myself in such a frustrated state, that I could not think rationally. It really was a sickness that I carried for so many years.

PLEASE DO NOT BLAME YOUR PARENTS

When I think about all the problems and trouble I experienced over the past thirty years, I must take responsibility for my actions. However, I want to acknowledge that the life experiences we have each lived does have an impact on us. We can react positively or negatively, but the fact remains that our history and family life are part of the life equation. Although my father is doing great now and serving the Lord Jesus, there was a time when alcohol was winning the day. This ever-losing battle with alcohol caused a lot of harm and eventually destroyed our family. And although this is true, I still have many wonderful memories of my childhood. When my parents divorced, I told myself that this would never happen to me. I was going to do it right. I was going to show people that I could be a success. I was going to show people that I didn't have to be a statistic. The impact that this alcohol and then divorce had on me was tremendous. It cannot be overstated how my attitude and countenance changed. Years later, after my own divorce, my childhood friends recalled how much I changed during that time in life. I was so fearful of having the same outcome that I eventually did indeed have my own downfall. So do I blame my parents? No. Did that time in their lives affect me? Yes. But I love my parents and realize they were doing the best they knew how at the time. So

I think each of us should acknowledge our past. It is good to recognize why we might have some of the habits, thought patterns, and behaviors we do. But it is never good enough to blame someone else. Their mistakes are past. They are forgiven. The question then becomes what will I do with my habits, patterns, and behaviors. In this day and age of a lack of responsibility, we must take that responsibility back. Let's commit today to take it seriously and let God move in our lives. Regardless of what your past has been, please commit today to move forward.

FAITH IN THE GOOD TIME, BUT FOR HOW LONG?

I have very fond memories of early morning prayer times at a church I used to attend. Very early on Saturday mornings, I think around 5:30, a group of men would meet in the sanctuary and each would generally take a usual spot as was their habit. On cold mornings, one of the men would fire the heater in the basement. It was quite comfortable to be setting in the sanctuary listening to the warm water run through the creaking radiators. It was such a pleasant and soothing sound. We would sit there for nearly thirty minutes, each man in his own place, praying to the Lord and seeking God. After some time, we would convene together and begin to speak words of encouragement to each other and/or share a passage of Scripture we had been looking at. Honestly, for me not being a great early morning person, it was difficult making these meetings. But once I was there, I was always thankful for the warm prayer time and good fellowship. I would have to say that I always left those prayer meetings with my mind clear and heart full. But … you know it has been said the truth always comes after the "but".

Why I am writing this? Because, it was often the case that after I left the church with a full heart and clear mind, that I was quickly distracted. It is amazing how quickly the mind will take on such worldly thoughts. Or thoughts of anxiety and worry. During the prayer time I was doing great, but then after getting home, I often fell into trouble again. Trouble in my thought life and back into discouragement. It was as if I had already forgotten all the wonderful things of the prayer meeting and was back running on my own pitiful strength. But I had to keep going back to what the Word of God said. I was forgiven. I was not a failure. I was redeemed and a new creation. Even though I would keep failing, I always believed in my mind that God's Word was true. Regardless of what the enemy had me thinking, I still believed it … even though I was not experiencing it. I like what Watchman Nee, the late Chinese pastor, said, *"Whatever contradicts the truth of God's Word we are to regard as the Devil's lie, not because it may not be in itself a very real fact to our senses, but because God has stated a greater fact before which the other must eventually yield."*

TIME DOES NOT ALWAYS HEAL A PROBLEM

Time goes on, and unless there is some radical change or intervention, our lives probably won't change. For someone caught up in a certain cycle or addiction, or maybe some way of thinking, it can be very frustrating. I found myself in a situation that I wanted to make better, but could never find the way out. It was so frustrating. I just wanted to quit and give up on everything. Bruce Olson, a missionary to the Motilone Indians in South America, experienced extreme discouragement and described it this way, *"What a filthy place! My chest felt tight. I closed my eyes to make it all go away. An old lady came out of the house and walked over to me, grinning a big toothless grin. She rubbed up against me in a friendly way, jabbering. She smelled bad. I looked at her tangled, thick black hair. Lice were crawling through it. Her breasts hung down flabbily. I stood up and walked from her, feeling sick. She followed, put her hands around my waist and hugged me. Then she laughed – a stupid lunatic laugh. I looked down at her hands. They were filthy. I gingerly took each one off of me and walked a little way into the jungle. She followed at a distance, giggling. I couldn't even tell her to get lost. A simple thing like that, and I couldn't say it. There wasn't a soul there who understood me. How long would it take? Three months? Four? Would I be able to communicate well within a year? There's an old gospel song that says, "If you can't bear the cross, then you can't wear the crown." I realized I didn't want the cross. I wanted the crown, with all its jewels, without ever carrying the cross. Looking again at the old woman, I wasn't even sure I wanted the crown."* We as Christians must make sure that we allow God to change us. Allow God to bring healing. Allow the process of repentance and regeneration to transform us. No, time does not always heal. Sometimes there must be an intervention. In Olson's case, God had to give him a supernatural healing and love for the Indians. He did, and to God's credit, a profitable Kingdom work was accomplished.

AN ADULT, BUT STILL ACTING CHILDISH

When our faith is weak and frail, it is as if we are like children. This can be good and bad. The Lord tells us we are to be as little children. But, in this sense, He is talking about our trust and dependence.

A young child is totally dependent on his or her parent(s) to take care of them. They cannot do anything for themselves so they act in trust that they will be taken care of. But when we as adults fail to grow up into responsible people, we remain childish. I can recall sitting in a pizza restaurant eating some dinner. Not too far from me was another table where a family was sitting. With the family were a couple of children. The older of the two children was probably ten or eleven years old. When their food arrived, the grandmother asked the older boy to eat his food. He immediately went into a temper tantrum and threw himself on the floor. He was yelling and kicking. The family must have seen this behavior before, because they did not looked surprised and just sat there. Everyone else in the restaurant was surprised though. Incredibly, this went on for several minutes. The thought of a person this old behaving in such a way was quite bizarre. When I think about that situation, it reminded me of my own tantrums. We must look the same way when we behave so childishly. Maybe not always to other people, but certainly to God. God wants us to examine ourselves, and then by the direction of His Word, start maturing into adults. How many times do we find ourselves figuratively throwing ourselves on the floor kicking and screaming because we do not get what we want. It is really a problem of self. When we behave selfishly, it is simply of manifestation of the self-life trying to take the throne. When we try to take the throne that only God deserves, trouble follows.

OUT OF THIS DEPRESSION AND DISCOURAGEMENT

I knew there was a way out of my depression and discouragement, but even with that, I wanted to do it my way. I always thought I had the best answer. And I was never shy in sharing it with others. I now cringe at the thought of how I must have made people feel. If the truth be known, they probably really didn't care to be around me much at all. And how could I blame them for feeling that way? No one wants to be around a person like that. At least not for long. Thinking about the pride and arrogance I exhibited in my speech and actions now makes me sick. Unfortunately, instead of pointing people to Jesus, my actions probably had the opposite effect. There had to be a process of humbling. That process is one of humiliation. I don't think we often think of humiliation as a good thing, but in my case it certainly was. And for the person that truly wants to live a life for God, this process of humiliation is necessary. Hopefully, it will come easier for you than it did for me. In the sixteenth chapter of Luke we read, *"And He said to them, "You are those who justify yourselves before men, but God knows your hearts. For what is highly esteemed among men is an abomination in the sight of God."* I always thought this verse was for those "other people" that needed my answers and input. But the reality showed that I was the one that needed adjustment. I was the one that was using my own Chris philosophy. It was as if I had created my own religion using passages of Scripture I wanted to use to prove my ideas. At the time I thought I was right. But now, I look back and realize that Jesus was not always the motivating factor in my life. I was trying to work things out with my own understanding. And when I did this, my depression and discouragement would only get worse. Yes, God knows our hearts. And He certainly knows mine. It is my prayer today as I come before the Lord, that my heart would be motivated by His ideas and not mine.

CAUGHT UP IN CYCLES OF LIFE

If you find yourself caught up in a vicious cycle of failure, then please know that you are not alone. Many of us have been there, and at times, thought there was no hope for success. But please know there is nothing wrong with you that cannot be fixed. God is in the healing business and He wants to heal you. When I think back to all the trouble I had before, it is evident that I was in bondage. Maybe you have an anger problem, maybe a chemical addiction, maybe a sexual addiction, maybe you love yourself so much it has manifested into extreme selfishness. Regardless of what your cycle of bondage may be, one thing is certain; it comes from the same root. Ultimately, our issues stem from a lack of total dependence on Christ. For me, it was a cycle of fear, control, and anger. It was a bondage because I kept doing things I didn't want to do. And when I acted angry or got upset, it brought on tremendous guilt and shame. This guilt and shame is exactly what the enemy wanted me to feel. When we feel hopeless, it completely disregards the hope that is found in Christ. Certainly, this is where the devil wants our thoughts to stay. However, there is victory in Jesus for those that will turn to Him and repent. Repent is not a word we hear often, but it is a word that needs to be preached and talked about more. If you are caught up in a vicious cycle of failure, then please take an examination of your life and ask the Lord where your life needs changes. In my case, I was lacking in accountability, and therefore, did not ask for help. I believe if I would have confessed my issues earlier, many problems could have been averted.

CHAPTER 3:

THE PROCESS

For pain and suffering that I caused
There were moments of fear all was lost
But the Redeemer had a heavenly plan
To restore and reconcile this sinful man

I WAS IN A STATE OF SHOCK WHEN I WALKED THROUGH
the living room and into the kitchen. The house was silent. As I
walked into the kitchen, I found a notebook on the counter. It was
open to a note telling me I was now alone. As I read the note over
and over, the reality set in that this was really happening. I then
picked up the notebook and walked through the sitting room into
the bedroom. As I stood by the bed, I had an overwhelming sense
of peace come over me. I did not hear God in an audible voice,
but quietly in my spirit I heard, "Chris, I am going to heal you
now." At that point, I felt not a hint of anger or despair, but rather,
a feeling of relief and joy. It wasn't joy because my wife had left,

but joy because I knew God was going to do a work in me. What I had wanted for so long, would now happen. It just wasn't how I thought it would happen.

I AM STILL ALIVE

In the book Robinson Crusoe, we find the following excerpt, "*It is not easy for anyone who has not been in the like condition to describe or conceive the consternation of men in such circumstances. We knew nothing where we were, or upon what land it was we were driven; whether an island or the main – whether inhabited or uninhabited. As the rage of the wind was still great, though rather less than at first, we could not so much as hope to have the ship hold many minutes without breaking into pieces, unless the wind, by a kind of miracle, should turn immediately about. In a word, we sat looking upon one another, and expecting death every moment, and every man, accordingly, preparing for another world; for there was little or nothing more for us to do in this. That which was our present comfort, and all the comfort we had, was that, contrary to our expectation the ship did not break yet, and that the master said the wind began to abate.*" In the book, Crusoe was given another chance at life. I also had another chance at life. At this stage of the process, all I knew to do was call a couple friends and start talking about what was happening. Just like Crusoe, I sat there not knowing what would happen next. For me, the part of this process would be one of the unknown. And for something that liked to plan and control things, this was quite a frightening thought. I had to keep taking myself back to that word I felt I had received as I stood by my bed. Even when we get a second chance at life, doubts will come in. It is during these times, when we must remember the promises of God, knowing that He loves us more than we can imagine. I am thankful I am alive today to tell this story. There were times in my life though when things looked so dark, that I wasn't sure I would make it. If you are reading this and find yourself struggling with something to the point you don't know if life is worth living, please hear me – life is worth living … keep reading and trusting God will bring you through. If my sharing these things helps you to see hope in the midst of your storm, then praise God for that. You will make it!

MY FRIEND TOLD ME IT WOULD BE A PROCESS

A few days after the separation, I scheduled an appointment with my doctor and good friend, Brad. I can remember sitting in his office telling him about what had happened and confessing a lot of the events that had been unfolding over the previous months. At that point I thought all would be well and that my family would be re-united soon. After telling him a lot of the story, I will never forget what he told me. He said, "Well it is really early in the process." I found myself thinking, "Early in the process?" I was thinking this whole reconciliation thing would only take a few weeks. After I sought some counseling and did what I needed to do, then surely we would be back together again soon. Little did I know at the time how correct he was. It was early in the process, but that is not what I wanted to hear. Other people would tell me that too, but I really didn't believe them. I figured I had a better way and would break some sort of record. I thought to myself, "How could she not come back … I mean really?" Had people experienced this before and knew what was going to happen? I suppose I was disillusioned, figuring that against all odds, I would be the exception. All these people talked about some kind of a process … but I thought, "they just don't know my story will be different." They said I would have to wait. Wait for what I thought. Let's get this thing moving quickly … really quickly! But quick it was not. It was painful to experience all the changes that were taking place. I am thankful I had true friends that helped me through these most difficult times. At that time there was so much uncertainty, but one thing remained. I knew God was in the process of healing me, and that brought me comfort.

THE DEFINITION OF A PROCESS

On September 5, 2015, I traveled to Dallas with one of my daughters and her husband to surprise mom. While there, my brother Bryan was gracious enough to buy us all tickets to the Alabama – Wisconsin game being played in Cowboys stadium. Bryan's wife's parents went to Alabama in Tuscaloosa and are huge fans. After we all went to the game that day, I was really hooked. It was so much fun, and I immediately caught Roll Tide Fever. I am not a huge sports fan, but I am a fan of Alabama College football. And I think more than that, I am a fan of watching excellence and the mastery of execution. It is not just about the game, but the fascination comes in watching a team perform together better than most ever do. The dictionary defines process like this – A series of actions or steps taken in order to achieve a particular end. When I think about process, Alabama football always comes to mind. Nick Saban, one of the greatest college football coaches, refers to The Process quite often when asked about his teams' successes and consistent performance on the field. Similar to a fine orchestra, his coaching philosophy brings the players together in a magnificent way with consistency not often found in other programs. It is in this process of Saban's, that each player is trained to execute well in each play of practice and each play of the game. Whether ahead or behind in the game, the goal is to focus on the play at hand. When that is done, the end result will be good. For me, I was getting ready to go through a process of my own. Even though I did not know what that was, I knew I had to keep getting up each day. I had to go to work. I had to pay my bills. I had to do life. Sometimes I would just lay my head down on my desk or go into the bathroom at work and cry. But I kept going trusting the Lord would get me through.

The undefined process

While I was at work on April 24, 2015, there was a group of ladies that were quickly packing up the house, helping my ex-wife to make her departure. One of our good friends was there helping that day. I would later learn that one of her jobs was to tape boxes closed after they were filled. Apparently, she was so nervous, that she was taping both ends of some of the boxes closed before there was anything in them. Believe me, the fact that I can sit here and laugh while I type this is more than proof that a miraculous work was done in me. Prior to my transformation, this would have enraged me. But now, I can look back on it and laugh. To think of her taping both ends of the empty boxes is really quite humorous, but then again, you would have to know her. She is one of the most encouraging people I know. And I do not fault her for being there that day. Since that time, she has done a lot for me in the way of encouragement and I appreciate her family very much. A couple weeks after the separation, I asked her to stop by to discuss listing the house for sale. Shortly after the separation, I received word that my ex-wife had no interest in ever returning there, so it was time to sell. After she looked around the house and discussed listing specifics, we stood in the cul-de-sac in front of the house and talked for a while. I can remember telling her that I predicted our family would be back together in six weeks. She stood there with a smile on her face and said she really had no idea. And for her to have been so reserved was really saying something. Although being a super-encouraging person, she cautioned me not to get my hopes too high. I really didn't want to believe people, but from what they were saying, it was going to be a long process. And even with that, there was no guarantee things would work out. We are still good friends. I am thankful for the testimony that is being worked out day by day and thankful for people like her. It was early in the process and there was no clear or definitive plan.

HOW COULD ANYONE IMAGINE SOMETHING LIKE THIS?

Was I going crazy? That was not the case, but there were times I felt like it. When we are in the middle of a healing process, there is pain involved. When I was twelve years old, I was hit in the ankle by a baseball. While I was standing in the batter's box, I was hit by a pitch and it let out quite a sound. The result of that internal infection causing blow was a month-long hospital stay. The surgeon opened my bone and kept it open for that entire time to let the infection drain out. It was a painful experience. The infection could have killed me or taken my leg, was slowly being purged out of my system one slow day at a time. Healing can be painful. It often is. But the result is good. No, I was not going crazy. Rather, I was experiencing the pain of separation. The pain of realizing the consequences of my mistakes. And feeling the pain of a healing process that was out of my control. And that's just the way it needed to be … out of my control.

WHAT OTHERS HAVE GONE THROUGH BEFORE

The Bible says there is nothing new under the sun. In other words, people will have experienced what we are going through even though the specific circumstances may be a little different. Many people had gone through the adoption process, so I knew we could do it to. But that didn't mean it wouldn't come with some unknowns. Near the end of November 1999, I was in Moscow Russia. I can recall sitting in the lobby of our hotel discussing adoption cases with some other families and our interpreter. We were supposed to go to the Embassy the next morning to process our son's entry visa into the United States. It was sometime during that evening conversation that it was brought to our attention the Embassy was going to be closed. This presented a huge problem because our flight arrangements did not allow for another day and everyone was quite tired after the lengthy stay in Vladivostok. Nearing the twelfth day in Russia was taking its toll on everyone and the thought of having to re-book flights and pay for additional hotel nights was not a pleasant one. So I phoned our adoption director in Houston and asked her if she could do anything. She proceeded to call our local Russian coordinator and told him to take us to the Embassy anyway, to see if there was anything he could do. We went to the Embassy the next morning hoping something could be worked out. Our coordinator, Victor, phoned someone, spoke for a few minutes, and then we waited. It seemed to be a long time, but after a while, the senior immigration officer walked into our small, and quite cold, waiting room. What happened next, I will never forget. The immigration officer gave Victor a verbal chewing and literally screamed at him saying, "Never bring people in like this again or you will never step foot into this Embassy again!" He then asked him to leave the room. When Victor left the room, the immigration officer smiled calmly and said, "Now how can I help you nice people?" He was very gracious and processed our visa even though the Embassy was closed. He went on to explain that he just wanted the coordinators to follow the policies. I think Victor got the point, but we were very thankful for his consideration toward us. This was an experience I will never forget. I like policies and procedures. I am a structure guy. But in that situation we were completely at the mercy of that man. Really, we were at the mercy of God.

THE UNKNOWNS OF THE FUTURE

I once heard an evangelist talk about a man at whose funeral he had preached. He described the man as one that loved Jesus, but had never really trusted Jesus. And as a result, this man was in a continual state of fear and doubt. I believe it could be said that doubt and fear come in like a flood when we go against all worldly and practical thinking we have been trained and taught to live by. And this is certainly true when we fail to put our entire trust in the Lord Jesus. Even for me, at this point in my life, this can be hard to define. There is an age old question of what is my role in my faith-walk and what is the role of God. Am I to make my own way using my intellect and effort or does God make my way by trusting in Him? I am not a Bible scholar, but I have concluded that it is a combination of both. God has given me intellect and He has given me the ability to think and work. But when I put my full trust in Him, then something miraculous happens. The current problem or struggle doesn't always go away, but the stress and anxiety of the situation does. In my case, I was one that said he loved Jesus, but was never one to fully trust in Him. Maybe you can relate to this. If you have been struggling with a particular issue for some time, might it be fair to say you are not trusting in Jesus as you should? I do not know your situation, so you will have to decide that. But, I can speak for myself in saying that my trust was never what it should have been. And because of that I suffered from fear and anxiety all my life. And even now, after all the transformation I've been through, I have to decide whether to keep trusting Him or not. It is my desire to continue in Him. I don't want to go back to that old way. Now that I have experienced breathing clean fresh air, why would I ever want to go back to a smoke-filled room!

What was going to happen to me?

A pastor friend of mine would sometimes say, "That is not the hill I wanted to die on!" I like that statement. Even though we cannot control our circumstances, it speaks to our ability to choose. Somehow, within the miraculous cosmic realm of God's sovereignty, He has made room for us to make choices. Could that previous sentence be the one to end all Calvinistic Armenian debates? I think not, but at least it makes sense to me. While things were so rough in our marriage, I never really thought that divorce was an option. It was not even possible for me to think of such a thing. How in the world could that have been possible? In my mind, that was never a hill I could die on. I would die a thousand deaths of other causes before I could imagine that one. But that is seemingly the hill where I would fall. But upon further examination, that was really not true either. I died on my pride. I died on the lack of effort to make changes earlier in life. I died because I was not putting my full trust in Jesus. And because of that, I suffered a painful death. And a death that affected others. Well, that is kind of depressing, but the good news come next. Out of that death came life. Just like a seed having to die to bring forth growth and life, I experienced that very thing. It was not the hill I wanted to die on, but I did. And again, springing out of that death, I am thankful to have a new life to tell about it.

WHERE IS THE FINISH LINE?

Adversity is really the forgotten blessing. It is the forgotten blessing, because we don't give enough thanks for it. And whether one believes that adversity comes from the devil or God Himself, we should agree that adversity stretches us, grows us, and helps us to become the people God wants us to be. Understandably, no one I know enjoys suffering or pain. But it can have a purpose. When the separation occurred, I suppose I could have completely derailed from life and ended up in a bad way. But I am thankful to have taken God's path of transformation. When we find ourselves in a time of adversity, we are at a crossroad. We can take several directions. The world will certainly give us plenty of roads to take leading to destruction. But if we choose God's road, we will find peace and healing in the process. In my case, I firmly believe God's grace pointed me to His path and only by His Grace can I stay on it. In the midst of the storm, we have a choice. I pray as you read this, you will seek God's path for your life. If you are in the middle of a mess, what do you have to lose? Try God's way! I believe He will show you He is faithful and true

CHAPTER 4:

OUT OF CONTROL

Addiction of control brought anxiety so high
My life was uncontrollable I cannot deny
Into the darkest depths of despair I went
With confusion and torment my mind was bent

I WOULD SAY I HAD AN ADDICTION BECAUSE I KEPT DOING something I didn't want to do. Wanting to control things may not seem like an addiction, but when you continue to do something you don't want, it's an indicator of addiction. And because I could not break that cycle of failure and guilt, it brought on a lot of anxiety. It is amazing the places the mind can go. And in my former state of mind, I was feeling hopeless. In my case, hopeless to the point of wondering if life was worth living.

JUST STOP IT

There are a couple passages in the Bible that really point to the battle going on. This battle is often played out in our minds, but why? In Ephesians 6:12, we read the following, "*For we do not wrestle against flesh and blood, but against principalities, against powers, against the rulers of the darkness of this age, against spiritual hosts of wickedness in heavenly places.*" As you read this, you may or may not agree with what is written, but I believe it makes no difference. This is what is taking place. There is a spiritual battle going on, and for many years, I was losing the battle horribly.

All Scripture is remarkable, but what Paul writes in Romans chapter 7 is especially remarkable to me and something I can identify with very well. In verses 13-18, we read the following, "*Has then what is good become death to me? Certainly not! But sin, that it might appear sin, was producing death in me through what is good, so that sin through the commandment might become exceedingly sinful. For we know that the law is spiritual, but I am carnal, sold under sin. For what I am doing, I do not understand. For what I will to do, that I do not practice; but what I hate, that I do. If, then, I do what I will not to do, I agree with the law that it is good. But now, it is no longer I who do it, but sin that dwells in me. For I know that in me (that is, in my flesh) nothing good dwells; for to will is present with me, but how to perform what is good I do not find.*" Paul's passage hits on something very near and relatable to me. For years, I wanted to be a good husband, to be a good man, to be a strong follower of the Lord Jesus. But what I wanted to I did not do. And that which I did not want to do, I would do. This, in and of itself was very discouraging and depressing. Again, it felt like a prison that I could not get out of. I am thankful today He set me free from that prison. But I must continue the story.

IN DESPAIR

I really hope you have never experienced thoughts like this, because it is a feeling of complete desperation, loneliness, and hopelessness. I was caught up in a cycle of fear, control, and anger. Because I always lived in fear, my reaction was to try and control everything and everyone around me. Even the small things in life showed evidence of controlling behavior. I like how author Dave Harvey described some of his controlling tendencies. Harvey writes, "*But there was a kind of security and trust that I placed in the control that order facilitated. When that broke down, my cravings were agitated and my heart exposed.*"

Life eventually got to a point where I felt everything was out of control. I was having a lot of stress at work, I didn't like my ex-wife's job schedule, there was continuing problems with some of the children, one of my daughters was talking about marriage before I thought it was time, and my relationship with God was just messed up. All of this, much of it self-induced, was really wearing on me. Everything seemed out of control, and I found myself thinking like this: If I cannot be in control, then I really don't know how to live. And if I can't figure out how to live, then I would rather not live at all. This was how bad the control issue was getting. It scared me and it scared those around me. At least those living with me. Others in my life did not know what was going on inside of me. If only I would have sought out help sooner, maybe the outcome would have been different.

DECISIONS HAVE CONSEQUENCES

Part of my editing process for this book included spending weekends in Forest Park. I would usually take a bench by the lake and work for several hours at a time. On one occasion, I watched a man and his young daughter walk past me holding hands. I heard the man say, "We have to get you back to your mom's house soon." They were having a fun time, but it made me a little sad. I didn't know anything about them and will never know what went on in their lives, but apparently their family was not together. I can only speak for myself, but my decisions had consequences. The principle of sowing and reaping as seen in the Bible was true when Jesus was on the earth, and it is still true today. In Galatians 6:8-10, we see the following, "*For he who sows to his flesh will of the flesh reap corruption, but he who sows to the Spirit will of the Spirit reap everlasting life. And let us not grow weary while doing good, for in due season we shall reap if we do not lose heart. Therefore, as we have opportunity, let us do good to all, especially to those who are of the household of faith.*" Instead of sowing to the Spirit of God, I was constantly getting distracted and sowing into other things. The principle of sowing and reaping cannot be underestimated. And I have often said that there is not a neutral. Because if we are not sowing into things of God, then by default, we are sowing into ungodly things, as innocent as those things may seem. I was not doing my part in relying on the Spirit of God. And because of my lack of discipline in this area, consequences were rendered. We have a choice. Each of us has a choice to seek God each morning. My life has changed now. It is with appreciation and awe that I get up each morning, kneel down at the side of my bed, and ask the Lord to live His life through me that day. When I make the decision to do that, the results and consequences throughout the day are pleasing to Him.

THE ENEMY WAS WINNING

In the opening scenes of one of my favorite movies, *A Wonderful Life*, the angel Clarence is called to the task of helping George Bailey. Clarence is told that a man down on Earth needs his help. Clarence asks, "Is he sick?" And the answer he receives is, "No worse, he's discouraged." How true this is! Being discouraged has to be one of the worst feelings that we as human beings can endure. But it is also an indictment against us. Showing a lack of trust in our Creator God, we wander around aimlessly in the wilderness like the Israelites did in the Bible. We continue to try working and walking in our own strength. I was guilty. I was trying to work things out in my flesh but I was losing. God, in His Word, likens these misguided pursuits to whoring around. In all seriousness, God demands our devotion and surrender. When we are found absent from this, trouble and discouragement follow. Psalm 106:39-40 says, "*Thus they were defiled with their own works, and went a-whoring with their own inventions. Therefore, the wrath of the LORD was kindled against his people, insomuch that he abhorred his own inheritance.*" And then in Psalm 73:27-28 we read, "*For, lo, they that are far from thee shall perish; thou hast destroyed all them that go a-whoring from thee. But it is good for me to draw near to God: I have put my trust in the Lord God, that I may declare all thy works.*"

The real church is comprised of individuals wholly given to Him. These individuals have completely sold out to the Lord Jesus and have given their whole lives to Him. If we attempt to build God's house in our own strength, we will be found wanting, frustrated, and worn out. Not only this, but we will have built something upon a false foundation while giving ourselves a false sense of accomplishment. This is the state I kept finding myself in.

BREAKING THE ENGLISH FIGURINE

At some point, my ex-wife's grandmother had traveled to England with some friends and returned with a beautiful figurine of an English man and woman. It was a beautiful figurine that portrayed the two individuals as very innocent and full of life. It ended up in our home and sat on one of our dressers. During one of my less than happy moments, we got into an argument and I was absolutely livid. Mind you, it was probably not over anything that serious. But in the mental state I was in, I would just get very angry. As the ugly argument continued, I got more and more upset. I eventually raised my fist and pounded it down on that dresser. The figurine was on the opposite end, but when my clenched fist came down, it hit very hard. The figurine jumped off of the dresser about 6 inches and then hit the floor, breaking the head off of the man. It did not dawn on me then, but how fitting was it that the man's head came off. Because I was acting out of my mind. Well, with that, the discussion was very much over and there was nothing I could say at that point. She was scared. I picked up the pieces. All of this was happening at about 1:00 in the morning, but I got in my car with the pieces and drove to my work office about twenty minutes away. When I got to work, I found some glue in our die shop and sat at my desk gluing the pieces back together as good as I could. As I sat there at my desk, I just thought about what a fool I had been. Like a man without hope and not knowing what to do.

About two hours later I drove home and quietly went inside, put the figurine back on the dresser, and went to bed.

As usual, it took several days for things to get smoothed out in the house. But it was not long again until something else happened that upset me. These things are painful to write, but the memory is there. If it were not for the grace and forgiveness of God, I know I would not be here writing this now. About twenty years later, after the divorce and during the move, I ended up with the figurine. It was setting on a piece of furniture in my basement. At some point, one of the kids must have knocked it over. The next time I saw it, the man had been broken off. The woman was still standing, but the man was now separated and laying on the table by himself. I looked at it and had to smile. I thought how appropriate this is. I then got out some glue again and attached the man, and then returned it to her. The figurine stood witness to many things for those twenty years. If the figurine could talk, it would probably tell these stories better than I can.

WHEN EVERYTHING IN LIFE SEEMS OUT OF CONTROL

It was around the end of August in 2015 when Mom and I flew into Krakow, Poland. As we started our descent, I looked out the window. Taken back by what I was seeing, in the midst of the beautiful Polish countryside, I realized I was looking at Auschwitz-Birkenau. Surprised to have looked out at the right time, I hurriedly grabbed my camera before we passed and took a nice aerial shot. At the time we were traveling, it had been nearly 75 years earlier that the first Jews were transported to Auschwitz. 1.5 million would eventually be murdered on this site in one of the most terrible atrocities in history. Years earlier, I had also traveled to the Holocaust Memorial Center, Yad Vashem, in Jerusalem. I have always been intrigued by these events and am amazed at how people could do such terrible things.

I would venture to say that most things are relative. What may seem difficult to me may not seem very difficult to someone else. Depending on the experiences and upbringing we have had, our reactions to things might be much different. When I think about the people that suffered during the Holocaust, I can only try to imagine the pain and suffering they experienced. To have had their property stolen, their wealth stripped, and most painful of all, having their families torn apart is really unimaginable. So when I think of tragedy, the Holocaust comes to mind. So in no way do I compare what I went through to be anywhere near what those people experienced. But for me, my changes in life were traumatic. Experiencing life changing circumstances is not something we can really prepare for. But when everything in life seems out of control, all we can do is trust God to bring us through the other side. And then, what we do with the lessons we have learned is up to us. Because my life felt out of control, I went into deep despair and my mind was filled with torment. But again, God was gracious to me. He was gracious to allow me another day of life. Another day of life to see His goodness and start the healing process.

THE ILLUSION OF CONTROL

Why do we ever think we are in control of anything? For goodness sakes, we do not ever really own anything. Even if we have assets that are paid for, we still have to pay the government each year for our cars and for our houses. When you look at it like that, we are simply borrowing or using the property for a period of time. And so it goes with our own lives. Ultimately, God owns the time and we are simply fortunate enough to be using it. When our mind begins to think we are in control, we are completely off-base as far as trusting God is concerned. This does not mean we are not responsible to get up in the morning for work, for buying and cooking our food, for performing maintenance on our homes and vehicles, and for all the things necessary to function in life. But what it means is that this is God's creation, each of us are God's people, and He is in control. When I started yielding myself to that fact, the stress I had put on myself for so many years went away. I began to see that I could not control how other people behaved and reacted to things. I saw that people would make their own choices and treat me how they felt they should. What a relief when I finally realized I was not responsible for all of those outcomes. All I was responsible for was to rest and trust in the One that was my provider, protector, and Savior.

So when we think we are in control and are trying to work everything out in our natural fleshly strength, it pushes the work of the Holy Spirit to the side and renders us useless to His purposes. The great English missionary to Africa, C.T. Studd, wrote the following about this very matter. He said, "*How little chance the Holy Ghost has nowadays. The churches and missionary societies have so bound Him in red tape that they practically ask Him to sit in a corner while they do the work themselves.*" Studd's analysis is pretty telling and quite sad. And it is not just some churches and missionary societies, but I found myself doing the same thing.

ONLY GOD IS TRULY IN CONTROL

When I was a boy, I enjoyed going with my parents to their friends' homes for lunch on Sundays after church. At one particular lunch, I can remember two of the men telling about some Creationist meetings they had been attending. It really struck my interest and was the beginning of a life-long interest in the topic. When we look at God's Creation, I certainly give Him all the credit for what is in existence. Some may believe in cosmic chance, that somehow everything just flew together. But it just never made sense to me. If God created everything, which I do believe, then it only makes sense that He also controls everything. At least that is my humble conclusion. Many will argue with that idea, but I don't see how.

Robert Gentry writes, "*Evidently, many scientists are willing to accommodate God into science, provided His presumed activities can be fitted into their evolutionary framework. However, when unambiguous scientific evidence is discovered, which is incompatible with evolution and can only be attributed to God's creative power, there is a different reaction within the scientific establishment.*" Ultimately, God is in control of everything. Whether you believe that God allows things to happen or causes things to happen, or even a combination of both ... the same is still true. God is in control, and because of that, we can trust him. The question really comes down to this ... Will we?

TRYING TO MANIPULATE OUTCOMES
BY PREDICTING REACTIONS

Although I am really not a very good chess player, I am impressed by those who are. I am not much into playing games. It always seems like too much work for me. When I want to relax, I just want to do something without a lot of thinking. So I am impressed by those that enjoy pushing their mental capacities even in their time off. On a recent trip to Branson to visit my daughter Hannah and her husband Jamin, we were walking on the campus where they attended college. There was an old grain mill near the greenhouses on the campus. We stopped to look around and when we exited the building, they spotted a checkers set made out of tree branches and decided to play. I sat on a bench next to them and just watched. They seemed to be having such a good time, but I was not really interested in playing. But when I think about games and strategy, I think of a movie called *In Search of Bobby Fisher*. In the movie they show a young prodigy training under a chess-master. It is intriguing to me how the chess-masters can look at combinations and moves in dozens of different scenarios and outcomes. It's really a fantastic mind that has this ability. And I would add, a God-given ability to be that intelligent.

In my life, I would find myself trying to predict others' moves and reactions. But I wasn't that smart. It was really a form of control. When I found myself choosing certain times and words to approach people with, it was really a form of manipulation. Manipulation is really a sad thing. I found myself in this position over and over again. And when I would worry about the possible reaction of people, it only added stress to my life. Instead of simply approaching people with a thought or idea, I would try to imagine multiple outcomes of their reactions and then form my approach. It was really a sickness. It was a sickness that kept me bound with my own thinking while preventing God to do a greater work in my life. I write these things because I want people to see the depth of what my controlling nature was. This was a serious problem for me, and had a negative impact on those around me. My life was really a mess.

It should go without saying that some of the best moments in life are those that are completely unpredictable. When I look at the wonderful things I experienced over the past several years, I am amazed at where God has taken me and who He has put in my path. My former boss and I were traveling back from a trade-show in Taipei, Taiwan. The plane was a little late getting in to San Francisco and we found ourselves running through the airport. Being in a little better shape than Ray, I ran ahead to the gate. The plane was just backing away from the jetway when the customer service attendant radioed the cockpit on her Motorola. Amazingly, the pilot pulled the plane back up and had the flight attendant open the door for us. Now of course, this was prior to the events of September 11, 2001, so things were a little more flexible then, but it was an amazing and completely unpredictable surprise. We were thankful. The people on the plane didn't look too happy when we finally walked on, but we sure were. God will take care of us. Even when we think the plane has left and it is too late, He can still work. There was nothing I could have done to have made that happen. I just prayed for a good outcome, and the result was good.

GETTING UP WITH MOTIVES

I can honestly say I have never gotten up in the morning with the intention of doing something wrong. Certainly, I never woke up thinking about what mistakes I could make or if I could hurt someone's feelings. So for lack of a better way of saying it, I never got up in the morning wanting to be a jerk. But just the opposite was true. I wanted to get up and do good things. To be a good husband. To be a good father. To be a good employee. And most of the time these things did go well. The problem was in my inconsistency and lack of predictability when it came to my reactions to others. Andreas Kostenberger makes a good point in talking about family. He writes, *"Ultimately, we human beings, whether we realize it or not, are involved in a cosmic spiritual conflict that pits God against Satan, with marriage and family serving as the key arena in which spiritual and cultural battles are fought."* There was certainly a battle going on inside me, and unfortunately, I was not winning.

CHAPTER 5:

IDOL WORSHIP

Cycles of fear and anger certainly a sin
Looking to others for worth an idol within
It was only for Him to breathe life in me
Seeking satisfaction elsewhere an errant plea

HAVE YOU EVER UNKNOWINGLY LIKED SOMETHING SO much that you put it on a pedestal? And in some ways, maybe actually worshipped it? Or maybe that object of worship was a person? In my case, I found myself relying on a person to satisfy my inner needs. And when this didn't happen, I felt lonely and insecure. People can only be people. And all of us as people are imperfect. So when we look to someone else to fill the voids in our life, we will eventually be disappointed. It is so easy to become distracted and fall into this trap, but thankfully, there is a solution.

PUTTING OTHERS AND THINGS ON A PEDESTAL

When you think of idol worship, what comes to mind? Maybe images of some distant land or maybe you think about references in the Old Testament of the Bible. I have been to India five times and each time I traveled there I was amazed at how many idols of worship there were. I worked with a lady at an orphanage in India. She was a nice woman and a cared a lot about the children in her care. She was an important person in the Indian adoption circles and was respected by many people. On one of my visits, she had some cake in her office that had been left over from a party. While the two of us were visiting, she got out three plates and cut three pieces of cake. She cut one for me, one for herself, and cut another to set outside in the backyard. I asked her what she was doing, and she told me it was for the animals. But it wasn't just to feed some hungry monkeys, but rather, it was an offering to the gods. On another occasion, she invited me to her home for dinner. Being a wealthy woman, it was one of eleven homes that she owned around the country. While there, she gave me a tour of the house. Being quite proud of it, she showed me through every room. I distinctively remember in one room was an altar. There were many idols around the altar and incense burning. And in front of the altar was a very thin Indian man sitting in a meditation pose reading prayers out of a book. From what I understood, she had someone in this room every hour of each day, submitting prayers to these altars and gods. Several months earlier, she and I were in Houston together at the Indian Consulate having tea with one of the diplomats she knew. During that trip I was able to spend some time talking with her about religion. Even though we had some opposing views on faith, we had a mutual respect for each other as professionals and always enjoyed the time together. But, I always remembered those idols. God have mercy on us.

TRYING TO FILL THE VOID ONLY JESUS CAN FILL

Are you tired of trying to fill the voids in your life? It is as if we have gone to great lengths to create all sorts of systems to find relief. We spend our resources and energy, creating these systems, only to find the voids still there. We can be absolutely sincere, but still be misguided. I have been to Asia a few times, and during each visit I spent a little time walking through the various temples. The architecture and detail is simply amazing in those places. When you consider all the magnificent places of worship around the world, that alone should be proof that man was created to worship. What people are worshipping is another story, but the sheer magnitude of human effort and energy devoted to places of worship is a clear indication that our Creator God intended us to do so. As I walked through some of the temples in Taiwan, I watched many people, young and old, going through the religious rituals. These rituals were done in unison and with much attention to detail. I appreciate devoted people. But we should be worshipping Him alone. God desires we would look upon Him as our sole point of worship. When we are trying to fill a God-shaped void with anything else, it is as if we have created an idol.

In the Bible, idol worship is strictly forbidden. The Bible teaches us that God expects and deserves our sole devotion and we are to have no other gods before us. But when we start looking around at other things in the world, our minds can be tempted and distracted. We may even look at clear passages in the Bible and ask ourselves, "Does it really say that?" Robert Plummer writes, *"One may qualify and explain the text away until consciences are dulled into happy disobedience."* The greatest deception lies closest to the truth, and when we start trying to rationalize Scripture, we have already been deceived. We start trying to rationalize with our feelings instead of staying true to what the Word of God says. And the Word of God is quite clear on idol worship. We are to stay away from it. In my situation, I had turned my idea of family into some sort of idol. Certainly, that was not my intent, but when I look back on my devotion and behavior, that is what I was doing.

WHY DON'T I FEEL MORE LOVE?

There is a hole in each one of us, and my opinion, everyone wants to be a part of something bigger than themselves. God created us to be in fellowship with Himself. And when we are in right relation with God, we feel our security, our purpose, our acceptance, and our identity. In speaking about these basic needs that each of us have, Jimmy Evans talks about the principle of transference. Because each one of us has these basic needs, we will try to get them filled in some way. Instead of having God as our central focus and provider of these needs, the tendency is to transfer that dependence onto another person, or a group, or an organization, etc. And when that person or group lets us down, which they inevitably will, then we feel lost again. When we are trying to get a person or group to accomplish what only God can, then our peace will be temporary. This is what I had been doing in my life. By trying to get a wife to meet those needs, I continually felt rejected and lost. It certainly wasn't because that person wasn't good enough, but it is impossible for another person to fill places that only God can fill. The Bible says that God is love. So true love must come from the source of Him alone. But in my case, I had made an idol out of our relationship, and it was doomed to fail. Why? Again, people are just people. And each of us has limitations.

Making the right things the top priority

What is important to you? What is important to us will eventually set our routines, our habits, and our priorities. I have never accumulated much in terms of earthly wealth, but when I was younger, I thought that would make me feel complete and accomplished. There was a movie that I would watch quite often about Wall Street and making millions of dollars. I would envision myself in that type of position, acquiring many earthly things and living for the world. Several years later, while I was finishing my university studies, I took a job for a manufacturing company. This position allowed me to travel quite a bit, which I really enjoyed. During one of my trips to New York City, I distinctively remember sitting in a window seat. It was an early morning flight and the sky was mostly clear, but a few clouds were in the sky. It was really quite beautiful. About half-way through the flight, I had an incredible sensation come over me as I looked out of the window. I realized at that moment, I would never work on Wall Street. Instead, I would be doing God's work. This is not to say that working on Wall Street cannot be God's work, but at least it wasn't for me. When we allow God to be the center of life, then our priorities take on a whole new order. Some people talk about the New World Order, but we should really be focused on Christ's New Order.

When we awake to what God's Word is saying and His Word takes root in our souls, amazing things start to happen. Watchman Nee writes, "*As unbelievers we may have been wholly untroubled by our conscience until the Word of God began to arouse us.*" When this arousing happens, our perspective takes a shift and we start viewing things in a different way. Anything outside of relationship with Christ is idolatry, but when that relationship is restored, we can look at a passage of Scripture like this and rejoice. We read the following in Colossians 1:16-17, "*For by Him all things were created that are in heaven and that are on earth, visible and invisible, whether thrones or dominions or principalities or powers. All things were created through Him and for Him. And He is before all things, and in Him all things consist.*"

PASSING INTO DAILY DEATH

Even after my separation from my ex-wife, it took about three years for the lessons to really sink in. In the Bible, the first chapter of Galatians indicates that Paul was in Arabia for 3 years before his ministry began. There is some debate about this. Why was Paul there? Was he wandering around for that time? Or was he being spiritually prepared for the ministry God intended? It is an interesting question. But we know that he was there. For me, it took me three years to really accept the new life that I had ahead of me. For those three years, I kept thinking things would work out and that our family would be re-united. But it didn't and that is ok. I am satisfied with my life now. The lessons that I learned were hard, but now I have a bright outlook and am serving the Lord each day.

Sometimes we believe something just because it is what we have always been taught. But what if there is another explanation for things? What if our perception is changed and we start looking at our reality from a different perspective. Most have seen programs and read theories on the construction of the Pyramids. And even most casual observers have an opinion on how they got there. Here is an interesting thought. Could God have put the Great Pyramid in Egypt? And I am not talking about all the pyramids on the Giza Plateau, but specifically the Great Pyramid. Most look at it as a tomb...as a symbol of death and place of burial. But what if the original intent was that of life? I would not want to be dogmatic about this, but certainly the possibility exists that God put it there. If one believes that God could create the heavens and earth by the sound of His voice, would the possibility of setting stones in place on the earth elude this same Creator? Of the 9 pyramids on the Giza Plateau, the Pyramid Khufu is quite superior in its size and construction. When one walks around all the pyramids, they can quickly observe that the other eight seem to be attempts at duplicating the grandeur of the first. You know, Satan cannot create, he can only attempt to duplicate. And it seems he has successfully taken ownership of the pyramid symbol. But maybe we should look at it another way.

Why do I say all of this? We need to be open to look at things differently. In most cases, we have been trained from early in life, to put our focus and trust on and in ourselves. Then when problems arise, we want to look to ourselves or others to solve them. But maybe there is a different way ... to trust and obey in Jesus.

It is not just some cheap religious slogan or Christianese talk, but rather, a true and dedicated walk with the Savior.

When we die to idol worship, we are coming alive to worshipping the real. That real worship is the committed and wholehearted worship of the Lord Jesus. Paul talked about death. He said that he died daily. Paul was not experiencing a physical death, but rather a death to his personal wants and fleshly desires. By experiencing this type of death, he was coming alive to a life in Christ that gave him hope and purpose. And it wasn't as if Paul came up with this idea on his own. Rather, he was simply living in obedience to what Christ wanted for his life. We are also to die daily. We are to die daily to whatever idols we may be worshipping. Maybe those idols are material things. Maybe they are financial holdings. Maybe they are people. Or maybe we are simply worshipping ourselves. In any event, God wants our full devotion. And this leaves no room for idols of any sort.

MOTIVES TESTED

After my first year of college, I felt a bit confused about which direction I should take. I was uncertain whether I should have continued or not. As I was talking to my dad one day, he mentioned the military. And it didn't take long, and I was on a plane to San Antonio, Texas, having joined the Air Force. When one enters the military, there is a lot of re-learning that has to take place. I met a friend in the airport, and when we landed at Basic Training in the middle of the night, we both looked at each other and said, "What in the world are we doing here?!" It was quite a shock, but over the following weeks, the drill instructors would train us in a way, making us better for service. We were being tested, and upon our graduation, we passed the test. When we give our lives to Jesus, there will be re-learning and it will cause us to examine our motives.

T. Austin Sparks wrote, *"All of our motives will be tested by fire. Are we seeking personal influence, popularity, reputation, prestige, acceptableness, or success? We may think our motives to be perfectly pure; but not until we pass into daily death, death to any or all of the above, and find ourselves 'despised and rejected of men', our names cast out as evil, and a real hold-up (seemingly) of our work, do we really come to face the true person and motive of our having any place in the service of God."*

THIS WILL NEVER HAPPEN TO ME

The Bible teaches that our righteousness is as filthy rags. In other words, the Bible says we are inherently not so good. However, this is contrary to what most people are taught and what many believe. We are quite indoctrinated with self-training from early on in our lives. And when you listen to a lot of people talk about all the problems we are having in society, a common answer is usually presented. The idea usually promoted is the notion of self-improvement. If we could just improve the human self, then we could become a better functioning people. But, the problem with encouraging self-esteem, self-confidence, and self-pride comes when our trained mechanisms override dependence on God. Our confidence and dependence must be in the Lord.

Self-confidence is falsely anchored to the individual, and let's face it, we are not very stable or reliable. At least I'm not. But the Lord Jesus is the same now and forevermore. By replacing our self-confidence with Christ-confidence, the person realizes their worth, but also the source and purpose of their value. Because when we are putting too much value on self, we ourselves can become the idol. Certainly, we should love ourselves, but only as a manifestation of God's love within us. We were created by the Lord Jesus for His purposes. Our life is not our own. I pray this resonates with you, as it eventually did with me.

MY RING ALMOST SLIPPED OFF

When the wedding ring was placed on my finger, I determined it would stay there forever. It was a visual reminder of the vows that I had taken and the commitment I had to one woman. But with the anxiety I felt, it also took on another meaning. It seemed to take on a meaning of success. And really not so much success, but the idea of not failing. It was as if it was a symbol I was doing things right and my marriage would not fall apart. This in and of itself took on a form of idolatry. A few months prior to the separation, I was taking a shower and had a little too much soap on my ring finger. As I wiped the washcloth across my hand, the fabric grabbed the ring and slid it to the end of my finger. The ring nearly fell off, but I was able to catch it just before it slipped off. It was saved. I can vividly remember the anxiety that rushed through my body, and my heart seemed to jump a beat. I think you would agree this was not a healthy response and was actually a sad commentary on my mental state. The ring staying on my finger meant so much to me. But why? Certainly, it would not have hurt to have taken it off occasionally. Or in the case such as this, if it slipped off, it should have been no big deal. I write this to show the level of anxiety I experienced. When people talk about being in a prison or in some sort of bondage, I can definitely relate to them. Mind-tormenting thoughts like this are horrible. I could not find a cure. At least not at that time. But the answer was coming.

CHAPTER 6:

CONTRADICTION MAN

Uncertainty would always come through the door
Who would Chris be today, the stress was a chore
From spiritual desert bones so dry
The more I failed, the harder I would try

I HAD ALWAYS WANTED TO BE A CONSISTENT PERSON. Whether it was in my eating, my fitness, my work life, or my relationships. But unfortunately, my terrible mood swings kept my consistency inconsistent. Not only were these inconsistencies in my behavior stressful for me, but it had a terrible impact on those around me. For most people outside of our home, they didn't really notice it. But, for my family and a few close people, they knew I had some issues. And to make things worse, when I failed, the guilt was overwhelming. My fleshly effort to improve myself continually fell short, and I lived in a constant state of contradiction. I repeatedly found myself doing things I didn't want to do and living outside of the messages and lessons I preached. It was a terrible condition.

HAVING THE OUTSIDE APPEARANCE OF HAPPINESS

It was a beautiful day in Washington D.C. Our family had just spent a week in New York at a missionary training center and then drove to D.C. for some sightseeing. We had driven into Maryland the evening before and arrived at the hotel a bit late. I was up early the next morning. I am not usually a morning person, but I was excited to get out and see some things. I had been to D.C. a couple of times, but I felt driven for the family to see as much as they could. Why couldn't I have just let them sleep a little longer? Was cramming so much into each day really necessary? But, like most other times, I didn't really consider what they wanted. I figured I knew what was best for them. Everyone was reluctant to get out of bed, but I persisted that we should get moving quickly. So after some time, we headed out on the town. After several hours, we found ourselves standing at the base of the Washington Monument. Having walked around the Lincoln Memorial and the World War II Memorial, everyone was a bit hungry. A conversation then began about where to eat. Being a bit tired and testy from the short night and long week before, the conversation did not go well. If I recall, the argument stemmed from whether we should have eaten at a restaurant or at a simple hotdog stand. I will never forget the terrible argument and bad feelings that we had at that moment. What a beautiful place we were in. What a wonderful time it could have been. But the following hours would be another reminder of how my selfishness and anger would keep me in turmoil. On the outside, we all looked fairly happy, but on the inside, I had failed again.

How are you doing this morning?

I was often guilty of lying to people when they asked me how I was doing. It was usually the case, when walking into church on a Sunday morning, someone would ask me how I was doing. Instead of telling them I was having a bad day or that I needed some prayer, I would just lie and say, "Doing great!" How often has that happened? And when that happens, an opportunity is lost and the chance for confession and prayer is missed. I found myself doing this a lot. I am not sure if it was due to pride or maybe I thought they really didn't want to hear about my problems. However, it is my hope now that each of us would take those opportunities seriously and open up with each other. If not with the corporate body, then at least a few in our inner circle that we can trust and rely upon. So the next time someone asks me how am I doing, I will tell them the truth … good or bad. And chances are, they will need some help as well. Because I was failing so much in my personal life, I think I was embarrassed, and a little fearful. It is sometimes hard when we don't know how people will react. But ultimately, I do believe people care and I should always be courageous to share my struggles.

Does it seem strange that it takes more skill and training to get a driver's license than it does to get married? Most of us were so unprepared. Yes, putting an untrained person behind the wheel of a car can be quite dangerous. But, could we also say that two unprepared people entering into marriage could also lead to trouble? The scene of a wedding is usually one of beauty and bliss, but maybe it would be more accurately depicted by showing two broken people at the wedding altar. What would people think if the groom showed up with cuts and bruises all over his body while he limped his way to the altar? And then to the crowd's surprise, the bride would walk down the aisle in a similar condition. I understand the wedding ceremony is to be a picture of Christ being gloriously united with His church, so I hope you understand my illustration. The fact is, we are all broken people without Jesus. And when we come into relationship with each other, there will be plenty of problems. So, we stand at the altar bruised and battered, and pray that God will make us into the people he wants. If we could only learn these lessons on the front-end of marriage before so much trouble surfaces.

OUR FLESH IS ROTTEN TO THE CORE

In one of his YouTube videos, counselor Allan Robarge said, "*If we don't make these changes, our relationships will be cycling and recycling in some toxic dysfunctional unsatisfied frustrating tension.*" My goodness … how true! I knew that from experience. But how to experience real change is the real question. Was it in my fleshly effort and will power that change was possible? No, it was not. Watchman Nee very poignantly wrote, "*However educated, however cultured, however improved it be, flesh is still flesh.*"

Not long after the World Trade Center attacks, a friend and I, along with our pastor, were there looking at the piles of rubble. We talked about the events of that day and what we thought might be some ramifications of it, but more so than that, we discussed the spiritual implications. It is a fact that the nation saw a lot of prayer after the Trade Center attacks of 9/11. We saw members of Congress out on the Capitol steps and observed churches packed by the thousands. Candlelight vigils were held around the country and many prayer services were held. Probably the most prevalent theme in the aftermath of those events was pride. Pride in the strength of our nation. Pride in our resolve. Pride in anything people could put their faith and trust in. But I believe this type of pride is what makes the Lord sad. Some took this as time for true repentance for our nation's sin, while others missed it all together. We had a great opportunity, through the shaking of the Lord, to seize a time of repentance. But instead, we went the other direction and staked our claim on the mountain of pride. When we put confidence into our flesh, we may find temporary victory, but it will soon dissipate.

IF I JUST TRY A LITTLE HARDER

I am not sure why I always thought I could overcome my problems in my own strength? After all, I was a Bible-believing Christian and should have known that was not possible. But still, the flesh would often win the day. The Bible says that our flesh wars against the Spirit. My goodness, how I know this to be true. Graeme Goldsworthy writes, "*If we constantly tell people what they should do in order to get their lives in order, we place a terrible legalistic burden on them. Of course we should obey God; of course we should love him with all our heart, mind, soul, and strength. The Bible tells us so. But if we ever give the impression that it is possible to do this on our own, not only do we make the gospel irrelevant, but we suggest that the law is in fact a lot weaker in its demands than it really is. Legalism demeans the law by reducing its standards to the level of our competence.*" And that is precisely the point ... I am not competent, and neither is anyone else. Oh yes, our flesh may be able to hang on for a period of time ... But, God wants our full dependence on Him. Anything other than that is unsustainable. We will eventually loose the grip we have on whatever we are struggling with. For me, it was this inconsistency that kept my family in uncertainty and fear of another outburst.

When I would fail, the guilt was so overwhelming. And then I would determine to do better. I really wanted to be a good man, a good husband, and a good father. However strong that desire may have been, it would always succumb to failure in the flesh. It can be hard to write these things, admitting that I had so many issues, but it is the truth. We can be persistent in our pursuit of a goal, but if was never grounded in any possible reality, then we are delusional. I was delusional to think that by trying to improve my flesh, I could find the peace I needed.

ULTIMATELY IT WAS A LACK OF TRUST

The sin of worry is what keeps our trust diminished and clouded by doubt. What are we always so worried about anyway? Do we not trust the God in Heaven that created us? When George Muller, the missionary to orphans in England, heard people talking about worry, he said, *"Many people have commented that such a way of living must cause the mind to continually think of how to obtain food and clothes, and thus become unfit for spiritual work. I answer that our minds are seldom concerned about the necessities of life because the care for them is laid upon our Father. Because we are His children, He not only allows us to do so but wants us to do so."* Muller knew from experience that his trust in the Lord to provide his needs would be prove faithful. And as a result, Muller ministered to thousands of orphan children. His biography is quite something to read if you have the time. At the end of his life, he monetary and earthly wealth was quite miniscule, but he had literally saved thousands of people through his ministry. Will you trust Him today?

LOST OPPORTUNITY

At some time after the separation, I started going to a counselor. But I was so fed up with things. I told one person, "I spent $1200 on this counseling and all I got was another kick in the teeth!" It goes without saying, I was probably not ready at that time. I was trying to prove to everyone that I had a better way; I just didn't think it was necessary. What was at the root of all this? It was really pride. Years earlier, I had missed another opportunity. At the beginning of the movie, Out of Africa, Meryl Streep's character Karen Blixen is narrating and says, "*I had a farm in Africa, at the foot of the Ngong Hills.*" Karen Blixen's home, just west of Nairobi, is still there and was the setting for several scenes in that movie. While I worked in Kenya, my office at the Tumaini Counseling Center was just a few miles down the road. So, I would jokingly tell people, "*I had a job in Africa, at the foot of the Ngong Hills.*" It was a beautiful compound of lovely buildings, well-manicured gardens, and many exotic birds in the trees. And at least several times a week, I would set potato chips on the window ledge looking out over the gardens, and then watch the small monkeys come and enjoy their snacks. I cannot say I was 'suffering for Jesus', but it was still missionary work all the same. I was the general manager of the counseling center. In my role, I managed the facilities, the budget and finances, and the Kenyan staff that worked on-site. My co-workers were coun-selors and doctors from all over the world. They were Christian missionaries that came to serve others serving in various parts of Africa in very difficult situations. They also helped people that had experienced trauma on the mission field and those that simply felt the stress of living in very harsh conditions.

So the entire time I was there, while still carrying my inter-nal issues and baggage, I missed an opportunity. I missed the opportunity to sit down and get some help from those very wise and dedicated people. What a shame that my pride kept me from humbling myself before them and admitting my faults. They were such kind people and were there to help. But again, I put on a good front, not wanting people to know all the issues I had in my life. So at the expense of my mental well-being, and that of my families, I stayed to myself. Several years after I left Africa, I wrote to some of those counselors, and asked their forgiveness for not asking for help. They were gracious and forgiving. It would still be many years later until I finally sought help and healing.

LET'S GET HONEST WITH OURSELVES

There is a saying that says, "Sin takes you further than you want to go and keeps your longer than you want to stay." When we have issues in our life, it is so important we confess those things and get the help we need. Instead of being prideful, it would be so nice to simply reach out for help. What a difference it would make in our life and those around us. But the good news is that once we get honest with ourselves, we don't have to do it alone. The path of repentance, confession, and healing is one we walk together. The

Lord says he has won the battle. We simply have to yield to Him and let Him do the work. II Corinthians 10:4-5 says *"For the weapons of our warfare are not carnal but mighty in God, for pulling down strongholds, casting down arguments and every high thing that exalts itself against the knowledge of God, bringing every thought captive to the obedience of Christ."* What it really comes down to is a state of humility. When we humble ourselves before our Creator, He can begin to work in us. When it is His work, we know He can then say, "It is good."

WHO DO WE REALLY THINK WE ARE?

I had just finished having dinner in the Old City of Cairo and needed to get back to the hotel in Giza. It was getting pretty late, but I found a cab. I had waived over several cabs prior to that, but they wanted to stay local and didn't want to make the longer drive to Giza. Once in the cab, the driver needed to stop for gas and I went into the shop to buy a bottle of water. Once settled back in the car, we started our thirty minute journey west. When we were driving over the Nile River bridge, I heard what sounded like a running horse. Before I knew it, a horse pulling a wagon was actually passing us on the bridge. Surprised, I just sat there and watched as a man was laying on top of a pile of watermelons. He was stretched out as far as he could extend himself, trying to keep control of the melons, and not lose them. It was late and dark, so it wasn't long before I lost sight of them. As we drove on, I wondered what kind of life they must have lived. I had just finished a nice dinner and was heading back to my comfortable hotel. But what about them? Rushing through the streets of Cairo on horses to get produce to its destination. I think they must have a hard life. Seeing things like this has always humbled me. We need to humble ourselves.

When I think about Cairo, I have great memories of talking to several men that helped me with tours and others that worked on the Giza Pyramid Plateau. One young man was named Islam. I had met him one day while trying to buy some water. There was a little girl selling some water near the base of one of the pyramids. I was out of money and she did not speak English, but I really needed some water badly. I went over to Islam and asked him if he could translate for me. He assured the young girl that I would come back in the morning with her money and a little extra for helping me out. She agreed and I was the owner of a new thirst-quenching bottle of water. Islam and I then took our drinks and headed for some shade under the shadow of one of the temple ruins. We had a great talk and I shared the Gospel message with him. It was a wonderful afternoon sitting there telling him about Jesus as we drank a cool drink and watched all the people touring around the pyramids. When we humble ourselves, God can work through us. I am not sure what eventually happened with the young man Islam, but I trust God used our conversation to encourage him.

WHEN WE ARE SPIRITUALLY SICK, JUDGMENT IS INEVITABLE
But when we fail to humble ourselves, we find ourselves in a terrible predicament. A predicament of which God must disciple and correct. In speaking of the nation of Israel, Warren Wiersbe wrote, "*From the human point of view, the nation was prospering; but from God's point of view, the nation was like a wretched victim who had been beaten from head to foot and left to die (Isaiah 1:5-6). The*

wounds had become infected, the whole body diseased, and nobody was doing anything to help. The false prophets and hypocritical priests of that day would have challenged Isaiah's autopsy of "the body politic," but the prophet knew that his diagnosis was true. In spite of the optimism of Judah's leaders, the nation was morally and spiritually sick, and judgement was inevitable."

What Wiersbe writes is so true. Just as Isaiah knew the Lord's judgment was coming, we can also know that our judgment is coming. When our bodies are sick, our systems will break down. When our hearts are sick, our families will break down. When our governments are corrupt, our nations will break down. But it doesn't have to be this way.

CHAPTER 7:

CONSEQUENCES RENDERED

Only God can help you she would say to me
But I was not advancing so she had to flee
What courage and faithfulness it took
It was a wake-up call to make me look

WORDS AND ACTIONS HAVE CONSEQUENCES. THERE IS REALLY no way around it. We are either having a positive effect or a negative effect. Unfortunately, there really isn't a neutral ground. Have you ever been given plenty of warning to make some changes, but didn't take the time or effort to do so? If you are like me, you would probably like to go back and change some things. But all we can do is move forward. And while we are making our choices, others will make theirs as well. This is what happened to me. I was making a lot of choices, and they weren't always good.

WHAT WILL IT TAKE TO MAKE A CHANGE?

Graeme Goldsworthy writes, *"We may achieve the outward sem-blance of conformity to the biblical pattern, but we do it at the expense of the gospel of grace that alone can produce the reality of these desirable goals."* Without the Prince of Peace, there will be no true lasting peace. This not only goes for the world and its nations, but also for us as individuals. The search for contentment that all of us are seeking shall be found in Christ. Isaiah 9:6-7 says, *"For unto us a child is born, unto us a son is given; and the government shall be upon his shoulder; and his name shall be called Wonderful, Counselor, The might God, The everlasting Father, The Prince of Peace. Of the increase of his government and peace there shall be no end, upon the throne of David, and upon his kingdom, to order it, and to establish it with judgment and with justice from henceforth even forever. The zeal of the Lord of hosts will perform this."* In the second chapter of Revelation in His letter to the church of Ephesus, the Lord Jesus reveals a sobering fact about that church. He tells them that even though they are doing some good things that they have lost their first love. *"Nevertheless, I have somewhat against thee, because thou hast left thy first love. Remember therefore from whence thou art fallen, and repent, and do the first works; or else I will come unto thee quickly, and will remove thy candlestick out of his place, except thou repent."* I am not sure who could end up reading these words, but let me ask you this …. Have you lost your first love? Have you lost that desire to seek Christ for your only source of true Peace? It is time to turn to Him.

IS THIS REALLY WHAT I SIGNED UP FOR?

The opening to the movie, The Ten Commandments, is quite extraordinary as Cecil B. Demille walks onto the stage and narrates the following, "*Into the blistering wilderness of Shur, A man who walked with kings, now walks alone. Torn from the pinnacle of royal power, stripped of all rank and earthly wealth. A forsaken man, without a country, without a hope. His soul in turmoil, like the hot winds and raging sands that lash him with a fury of a taskmaster's whip. He is driven forward, always forward by a God unknown, for the land unseen, into the molten wilderness of sin. Where granite sentinels stand as towers of living death to bar his way, each night brings the black embrace of loneliness and the mocking whisper of the wind. He hears the echoing voices of the dark. His tortured mind wondering if they call the memory of past triumphs or wail of foreboding disasters yet to come. Or whether the desert's hot breath has melted his reason into madness. He cannot cool the burning kiss of thirst upon his lips nor shade the scorching fury of the sun all about his desolation. He can neither bless nor curse the power that moves him for he does not know from where it comes. Learning that it can be more terrible to live than to die He is driven onward, through the burning crucible of desert where holy men and prophets are cleansed and purged for God's great purpose. Until at last, at the end of human strength, beaten into the dust from which he came, the metal is ready for the Maker's hand.*"

Moses was certainly tried and prepared for a greater work that God intended for him. Sometimes we are surprised, and maybe even shocked, at the condition we find ourselves in. But praise God that He is working in us for a greater purpose. Is my current situation one that I signed up for? Not necessarily, but I know I am a better person as a result of it. And now, I pray my testimony can be of some encouragement to others.

CONSEQUENCES RENDERED

It was near the end of August in 2016 when Mom and I were traveling from Salzburg to Rome in a comfortable sleeper car. We were about halfway through our Europe trip and were really enjoying ourselves. I had never been on a train before, and this was such a nice experience. When I booked the tickets, I paid a little more for the private sleeper cabin with its own bathroom and shower. As I recall, the cost wasn't too much more, and I really wanted us to be comfortable. Mom and I had not always had the greatest relationship, and so in some ways, I suppose I was trying to make up for lost time. Even after the trip, she would comment to so many people about how much fun she had. She was also impressed at my ability to coordinate and organize the entire trip. People asked her if we were on a guided tour, and she would always brag on my planning ability. It made me feel good. The train we were on left Salzburg late evening and would arrive in Rome early the next day. They served us a nice meal and then we had some coffee. We both enjoyed the comfort of our bunks while we read and did some journaling. I enjoyed the slight sway back and forth as we entered and exited the train stations. During the train ride that night, something was taking place back in St. Charles, Missouri. At some point while we slept that night, a judge was signing the official divorce papers in the court. Upon returning home after our trip, I received the court papers in the mail and noticed the date under the judge's signature. It was that same night we traveled in that wonderful sleeper car. It is not as if the date was that important, but I have a curious attention to know where I was, and what I was doing, when certain important events take place. Why do I tell this? Because it is another example of God's grace. I was being taken through a process of healing and correction. And being the controlling person I was, I could not be given a choice. God knew I needed compassionate regeneration, and this was the method He chose to use. People will have opinions about the method being good or bad, but regardless, I am thankful to be where I am today. Some of the most painful things in our lives will yield some of the best results.

OUR WORDS AND ACTIONS MEAN SOMETHING

Our overnight train ride from Salzburg was a success in getting to Rome on time. We then left Rome on another morning train to Capri, where we spent three nights. Capri was where the Roman Emperor Tiberius had his luxury getaway palace. While we visited, I tried to imagine what it must have looked like during his time. It was during the reign of Tiberius from A.D. 14 through A.D.37 that Jesus came into adulthood, ministered to the multitudes, and was Crucified and Resurrected. I am thankful to have seen many historical sites around the world, and as I stood on this place over 2000 years after Christ, I relished in the moment. It was during our last evening on the island of Capri that Mom and I sat in the hotel room on our beds feeling very tired. At some point, I turned to her and said, "Do you think we should go home a day early?" She quickly said, "Yes!" We were both very tired as we had covered a lot of ground in those 10 days. We had a Vatican tour scheduled for the next day, but at that point I really didn't care. When you're tired, you're tired. I had wanted to see the works of Michelangelo for years, but was really too exhausted at that point to go. So I called the airline and they were gracious enough to move our departure date up one day without charge.

During our last day in Italy, we walked the streets of Rome, toured the Coliseum, and the Ancient Forum ruins. Seeing the Coliseum was really special to me. As I stood there and looked at what had been the floor on which many games had taken place, I could only imagine the noise, the carnage, and the unnecessary death that took place there. I bowed my head and said a short prayer as I thought about the Christians that had been persecuted in that place. The cruelty exhibited by many in the Roman Empire at that time was the result of wrong thinking and misguided intentions. Tiberius was said to have demanded divine worship of his statues and images, which left the Christians with a dilemma. But the true believers would not bow to this kind of ungodly behavior.

Our words and actions mean something. And when we are committed to something, our words and actions should show loyalty and priority to that something. I was fortunate enough in my life to get a wake-up call that enabled me to grow and be healed. God's words and actions in our life also mean something. When God is speaking and working in your life, take notice and listen. He wants something better for you. As powerful as the Roman Empire was at that time, the Christians still had a better future. As we look at the carnage and unnecessary death around us today, let us as believers keep our eyes fixed on the Lord.

A THOUGHT IN ITS FINAL FIXED FORM

Norman Grubb wrote, *"A word is a thought in its final fixed form."*
When I think about his statement, it makes me think of Jesus.
We are told in the book of John that Jesus is the Word. And that
the Word came in the flesh. Jesus also serves as a part of God the
Father's finality … this conclusive and definitive finality to end all
sin struggles and curses. There is a fascinating verse in Scripture
that takes place shortly after the Resurrection of Jesus. As Christ is
walking on the road to Emmaus with the two disciples, we see the
following words in Luke 24:27, *"And beginning at Moses and all the
prophets, he expounded unto them in all the scriptures the things concerning Himself."* As they walked along on that incredible journey,
I suppose he might have included the accounts of Himself such as
the picture of Him covering Adam and Eve's iniquity and shame.
Some would suggest that this animal covering may have been a
lamb. Maybe Christ would have told them the story of the Passover
and how the blood on the doors of the Hebrews represented his
life-saving Blood that was shed. Maybe he would have recounted
the historical account of Moses holding up the bronze serpent as
the only hope for those dying. Maybe he would have told the story
of Abraham and Isaac and how a ram was provided as a substitute
sacrifice. Maybe he would have told the story of Rahab and how
the scarlet thread outside her window was her salvation. Or maybe
he would have told them about why priest would sprinkle blood
on the Mercy Seat on the Day of Atonement. We see all of these
were pictures of Christ's salvation to come. It seems as though he
was giving them a comprehensive worldview to the practical and
quite spectacular meaning of the Word of God.

LEARNING WITHOUT TOO MUCH PAIN

Is it possible to learn without much pain? Yes, I believe so. But often our greatest lessons come when there is pain involved. I am a father of six children and as I look back on our lives, I am thankful for the time we have spent together. There were many good times, but also times when discipline was needed. I can remember how one of my toddler daughters would walk up to the television and want to touch it. All I had to do was look at her sternly and she would back away in obedience. However, another of my toddler daughters would do the same thing. But upon looking sternly at her, she would reach out and touch it anyway. It was at that moment that I had the opportunity to teach and discipline. I would promptly get out of my chair, take her away from the television, and tell her no. All children are different, but we all need some sort of discipline. A loving parent will certainly discipline their children in love to the degree necessary to train them. And if you are wondering … both of those girls turned out to be lovely young ladies. There is quite a remarkable passage in Hebrews 12:7-8. In this portion of Scripture, the idea of a loving father disciplining his children is described in a way that shows how serious God takes the matter. The passage reads, *"If you endure chastening, God deals with you as with sons; for what son is there whom a father does not chasten? But if you are without chastening; of which all have become partakers, then you are illegitimate and not sons."* Hopefully, we can learn our necessary lessons without too much pain.

ONE CANNOT LIE TO THEMSELVES

Why do we try to lie to ourselves? We may put on a good face and fool some people, but we can never really fool ourselves. I smile when I think of a line by Morgan Freeman in the movie *"Stand by Me."* Freeman tells a young student, *"Son, you can't kid a kidder."* How true that statement is … and we surely can't kid ourselves. Theologian and professor Malcolm Yarnell writes, *"The person who abides in Christ is a disciple of Christ, and that person knows the truth that makes him free. The person who is outside of total obedience to Christ, the truth in person, is a slave to sin."* When we have a sin issue, it is going to require our repentance, our confession, and the healing of God to make things right again. Fortunately, the work of Christ on Calvary has paid it all. When we try to hide our sin, we are only prolonging the eventual product of that spoiled root. But when we confess our sin, healing will happen … quickly! We can sometimes lie and fool other people to believing we are something we are not, but we can't lie to ourselves. If anyone knows who we are, surely it is ourselves. Each of us as individuals know what thoughts and issues we carry. And certainly God knows our inward parts! So even if we can get by faking people for a time, what are we really accomplishing. I was told I needed some help. And that was true.

THERE IS NOT A NEUTRAL

When our children were growing up, I took a really hard line on music and television. And the issue is not just this type of media, but really all content and influences in our life. I would always tell my son there was no neutrality in media. Either the media content was good for us or it was bad for us. Was it pointing us to Christ or was it pointing us away from Christ? Was it making us a better person or was it adding to our human problem?

Andrew Murray, the South African pastor and author, writes, *"It is a terrible and very serious thought that one can maintain the appearance of a Christian life – think one is trusting in Christ – while yet living with the world for self and the visible."* The issue of music and media in our life is still a mystery to me. I realize we are in this world, but we are not supposed to be of this world. So each person, upon reading the Scripture and praying to the Lord, will have to be led to their conviction on the matter. But I still contend that there is not a neutral. Our words, choices, and actions are either reflecting a life in Christ or they aren't. In my former life, I was making choices, and they were not always reflecting a life in Christ. As a result, consequences were rendered.

HOT OR COLD

When we are being stubborn, we find ourselves in a lukewarm state. It could be likened to the person described in Scripture that gets carried and tossed about by every false wind of doctrine. Scripture also describes this type of person as double-minded or unstable in all his ways. What a miserable state to be found living in. There is a telling passage in Revelation 3:14-16, *"And to the angel of the church of the Laodiceans write, "These things says the Amen, the Faithful and True Witness, the Beginning of the creation of God: I know your works, that you are neither cold nor hot. I could wish you were cold or hot. So then, because you are lukewarm, and neither cold nor hot, I will vomit you out of My mouth."*

HE SET HIS SATCHEL DOWN

When we are stubborn and continue to choose to do things our way, something has to give. Or when we refuse to confess our sin and we get comfortable in a lifestyle contrary to God's way, a correction will be necessary. Why? Because God loves us so much. A former pastor and good friend of mine, the late Ken LaRue, had a lot of good sayings. He would often say, *"He set his satchel down."* In other words, some people are so stuck in their ways and they are not going to change. Ken would also say, *"If we fix the fix that God has fixed to fix us, then God has to fix another fix to fix us."* Huh?! Take the time to read through that again several times and let it sink in. Have you ever thought about it like that? Are you trying to undo the fix that God has fixed to fix you?

CHAPTER 8:

PAIN AND SUFFERING

The course of action was radically drastic
However, the end result utterly fantastic
Such crushing pain there was no lack
But Jesus knew it would bring me back

THERE IS SO MUCH PAIN IN THE WORLD, AND ESPECIALLY in places like Sudan. While in Africa, as one of the general managers of the mission group I was with, I had the opportunity to travel with a crew to Southern Sudan. We had a working arrangement with Samaritan's Purse and were flying on their DC-3 that day. A couple of my friends from the mission were the pilots so they gave me a good overview and education about their regular routine. We took off from Nairobi with a load of supplies to take to one of the villages. After flying over northwestern Kenya, we arrived at our destination in Southern Sudan several hours later. The runway was a simple strip of dirt surrounded by scrubby brush and trees.

On our initial approach there were a few animals walking down the runway, so we had to make a quick and low flyover to startle them away. We landed the second time around and were then surrounded by people awaiting our supplies. It was my first time to experience something like this. To see so many people dependent on the supplies and living in such poverty was quite a humbling experience. After unloading and parking the plane, we were picked up by a UN employee in a Toyota Landcruiser. He took us to a tent camp where we enjoyed a nice meal and fairly-comfortable tents with bunks. I took a quick shower and then crawled into bed under the mosquito net and tried to get to sleep. The entire experience made me appreciate more what the Sudanese people were going through. There was a lot of pain and suffering in that place, and it showed on the faces of the people. It was great that we could be there to help, but there was so much need. I can only imagine the pain they may have faced.

PAIN OF MENTAL ANGUISH

I suppose all pain is relative. Depending on what a person has experienced and how they have lived, situations will impact them in different ways. During the day after my separation, I felt mental and emotional pain in a way I never had before. It was so heart-wrenching that is was like a physical pain. Our emotions are quite incredible, and by the grace of God, He helped me through that very traumatic time. When I think about pain in a person's life, I remember a movie about the author C.S. Lewis. The movie *Shadowlands* was a great story concerning parts of Lewis's life. The movie portrays Lewis as one that had never wanted to be close to anyone because the thought of losing them was too painful.

However, he met a woman named Joy and eventually falls in love. He tried to keep his emotions in check, but she won him over with her strong personality and somewhat abrasive charm. Shortly after they fell in love, she was diagnosed with cancer. Shortly after her diagnosis they got married and spend quality time together with the limited amount they had left. It wasn't too long before she dies, and then the pain that Lewis had always feared set in. In one scene, he is sitting in his attic with Joy's son talking about her passing and then the emotion overwhelms him. At that point, he says a remarkable thing, "*The pain I feel now is the happiness I had before.*" It is quite a moment where the feeling of joy and sadness mixed together come over him in a way he had never experienced. I have thought of that scene over the years and can also relate to that. I don't think I had ever experienced such strong emotional pain such as I did, until my family was broken. We had a lot of good times together, but the brokenness was very painful.

I NEVER WANTED TO HURT ANYONE'S FEELINGS

I have always had compassion for people and have tried to help others when I could. So I certainly never wanted to hurt anyone's feelings. But because of my broken state, I kept doing that to people I cared about. And especially to my ex-wife. She certainly didn't deserve the up-and-down emotions that I constantly exhibited, but I could not seem to change myself. The whole process was quite painful. I have told people, "I never got up in the morning and wanted to make a mistake!" But for some reason it kept happening. What I came to realize was this. When I didn't get my way or when I started to feel insecure, the pain I felt inside would be projected onto other people. This entire cycle was painful for me and those close to me. Especially for those that loved me. This is why it is so important for us to acknowledge our issues, and then in repentance, ask God to heal us. When I look at people suffering from various problems now, I am sympathetic. I realize that their outward behavior and issues are really not how they want to be. They are simply acting out of their current heart condition. When our hearts are empty and void of hope, it is painful. And that pain is then manifested and projected. Hallelujah, we can have a better way to live.

WALKING INTO AN EMPTY HOUSE

Although I knew that God would use this painful process to correct and heal me, walking through an empty house was hard. For those that have experienced that, I feel for you. For those who haven't, please have sympathy for those that have. Up until that time, our house had been a very busy place. We had lived in the same house for twenty-one years and raised all the children there. I was used to coming home after work to my wife and six children. There was always something going on, and it was our usual habit to try and have dinner together at the kitchen table with the entire family. For all of our shortcomings, at least this was usually successful. It was a smaller house, so we were always together. We watched a lot of movies, did homework, went to softball games, and all the usual housekeeping and living involved with eight people. Once I was alone, it was such a strange feeling that I had never really thought about. It felt a bit awkward to walk through each room and experience the silence. I was not familiar with silence, but eventually got used to it. And now I enjoy it! But during those first months, it was very painful. The solitude that I experienced during those first few months would be used to bring me closer to the Lord Jesus. Call it what you want, but it was really forced quiet-time. It was a quiet time to be alone with God. Whether our pain is self-inflicted or forced upon us, we can be assured that God wants to mold us and teach us during those times.

WHERE IS THE HELP?

During that evening of April 24, 2015, two of my friends, Doug and Brian, stopped by to see me. I was a bit surprised that no one from the church called or stopped to check on me. People in the church knew what was going on because some of them had been there that day packing boxes, and one of the men from the church had called Brian to tell him what was happening. I would later find out that someone from the church had asked an off-duty police officer to watch the doors at the church, apparently worried that I would try to cause trouble during that evening's women's meeting. Several days later, after some of the shock wore off, I found myself thinking, "*If they were so worried about me harming myself, why would they not have checked on me? That is so strange!*" That was painful and I harbored some resentment about that for a couple months. Eventually, I worked through the process of forgiveness. The thought of causing trouble or chasing after my wife had not even entered my mind. Considering what was going on, I had no ill-intentions and was remarkably peaceful. I kept remembering that sensation standing next to the bed, as God spoke to my heart, "Chris I am going to heal you now." So I was relatively peaceful.

But I understand that others were uncertain, and honestly, they probably just didn't know what to do or how to react. I certainly wasn't prepared for a situation like this, and they weren't either. The Bible says that the wages of sin is death. I believe that not only means a physical death, but also a spiritual death. And when sin is in the equation, a lot of things just don't make sense.

HEY MAN, WHAT ARE YOU IN HERE FOR?

I remember telling Doug that night that I would be ok to sleep in the house alone. I was convinced that I had the good sense to get some sleep. And I was also convinced that I didn't want to harm myself. Being emotionally exhausted, I just wanted to get through the night. He said he would stop by the next morning. After making a couple more phone calls that night, I went to sleep, and surprisingly, slept quite well. The next morning he came over and brought a notebook and a journal. The counsel Doug gave me was fantastic. He sat at the kitchen table with the notebook and wrote out a couple dozen things that I needed to think about and things to help me keep perspective. He also gave me a few Scripture passages to help me. I told him that morning that I really wanted to see a counselor and get checked out. He called a treatment center and made the arrangements. Within a few hours, we sat in the lobby of the treatment center. He warned me that behind those reception walls, was a different world I had never experienced. He said it would be quite an experience. But I assured him I wanted to go through with it. At that point, I just wanted to lay in a hospital bed for a few days and let myself calm down.

It wasn't long, and they called my name to go. I thanked Doug for all his help and walked in. After having all my personal belongings and clothes taken, I was shown to a hospital room. It was a decent size and it was clean. I had a roommate named John. John was in the treatment center for the third or fourth time for drugs. I was laying on my bed, when he walked in the room. John was a tall man with longer hair and a mustache. He looked pretty frazzled and worn out. He sat down on the edge of his bed, looked at me, and said, "Hey man! What are you in here for?" At that point I quickly thought to myself, "I don't have to worry about hurting myself … this guy might strangle me in the night!!" So with that thought I said, "John, I have been reading my Bible this morning. Would you mind if I also read to you out loud?" He was agreeable, so I read out of the book of John, and for the next several days, we would get along fine. Over the next few days, I would have some good visits with my children and my pastor, and get some much needed rest.

There were people in that treatment center for a variety of reasons, but primarily emotional issues and drug problems. Even though I was going through a traumatic time myself, my heart went out to all the people I saw in that place. It was really my first experience with the "drug-crowd." I do not mean that in a derogatory sense, but I had just never ran with those type of people, so my exposure to those type of issues was very limited. I would start conversations with a lot of them during meal times and had some good prayer time with them. Honestly, I cannot say that I gained that much personally from being in that place, but I can say I grew in my experience with those precious souls. I experienced a level of pain in people that I had not known before. It was the pain of being trapped in an addiction they didn't want to have. But I had my addiction. An addiction of control … and it was painful.

Pain for the suffering I caused

God is loving and that means He will do anything necessary to teach and help us. But unlike so many modern definitions of love, His love is also one of correction and judgment. I believe it is important that we are teaching and preaching the entire Gospel. The entire Gospel is not only about the saving, but includes the repentance necessary for the saving work to be complete. The Israelites were judged for their sin. The Scripture says there is nothing new under the sun. And as far as our sin condition is concerned, that certainly holds true. The same selfish sin issues that we deal with today are no different than what people dealt with during Bible times. God gave the prophet Jeremiah a word that the Israelites would go into captivity because of their sin. Because they were not following God's ways, they were judged. The Lord was also very specific and told them it would be seventy years. As was the case with many prophetic words, the people just didn't believe. And over and over again they would fail the Lord and fall into sin. When the Babylonians eventually entered Jerusalem and took the people captive, I suspect the people were quite shocked. Should they have been surprised that God was really serious? Should they have been surprised that God wanted their true and undivided attention? Their faith and fellowship with God was lacking, and unfortunately, they missed an opportunity to repent and turn their hearts back to God. But later, as they sat in another land, thinking about the country and homes they were pulled from, they felt the pain of regret. This verse from Psalm 137:1 says, *"By the rivers of Babylon, there we sat down, yea, we wept when we remembered Zion.* It was a time of mourning, reflection, and reckoning. It is painful when we have to take responsibility and accept our discipline. I suspect most people really don't want to hear that, but it is true anyway. If we could only turn back the clock and do some things differently.

The Israelites didn't get to decide how and where their discipline would happen. And neither do we. It is painful to reach a point in life where we feel regret. And while we have to accept the mistakes of our past, we can rejoice as we look forward to our new life in Christ. Regardless of how old we are, we can take the opportunity we have with each day remaining. I am thankful I have new opportunities in life and I praise God each day for them.

SCARS TO PROVE IT

A good friend of mine is in the insurance business and he used to have a small sticker on his car door window that read, "Call me, I have the experience and scars to prove it." Life is hard at times. Life is unpredictable and often brings us to places of physical and emotional changes we didn't know were possible. When I think about scars and endurance, I think of Richard Wurmbrand who spent years in communist Romanian prisons. He and others endured incredible hardships and torture. Wurmbrand was one of those heroes of the faith that had actual physical scars. His scars were not caused by anything he did wrong and were certainly not from accidents. His scars were the product of his humble yet persistent obedience to preach the Word of God. His outspoken and unbridled preaching from the Bible landed him in some of the most difficult prison situations. And through it all, he maintained his faith and hope, and by doing so, had a tremendous testimony. Eventually, he could look back on some of the situations even with a bit of humor. Wurmbrand wrote the following, *"A number of us decided to pay the price for the privilege of preaching, so we accepted their terms. It was a big deal; we preached and they beat us. We were happy preaching. They were happy beating us, so everyone was happy."* Everything we go through in life has some effect on us. The trouble that I used to experience would certainly have an impact. It was painful for me and those around me. And there are some scars. Jesus had some scars too. Not because of anything He did wrong though. And that is what is so miraculous. Jesus took on scars undeservedly, to heal and cleanse me from the scars I deserved.

Will we learn from the suffering and pain?

God made us with such strong emotions and people are in all sorts of predicaments. People react and cope with pain in different ways. Some situations are more extreme than others. I can recall driving through Mexico City, and in part of the city, seeing the rows of prostitutes. My heart went out to these girls that seemed to have no hope. I asked my Mexican colleague how much the girls would charge, and he said about thirty dollars. I was shocked and saddened. To think of such a life of pain and suffering just to survive. Lord Jesus come back soon. For me, my pain came in a different way. I was experiencing pain from my regret and loneliness. But, God knew that is what I needed to bring me back. Michael Card writes, *"In the wilderness, the stark severity of David's life pressed him to make one of two choices; avoid the forsaken sense of suffering it causes and find a substitute for intimacy with God, or stubbornly refuse to let go of the loneliness and continue on the path toward an ever-increasing, continuously painful, unheard-of intimacy with God. David's two choices are still our only ones today."*

I Peter 5:10 reads, *"But may the God of all grace, who called us to His eternal glory by Christ Jesus, after you have suffered a while, perfect, establish, strengthen, and settle you."* This really is the goal. God took my pain and suffering and is turning it into something good. I pray the pain you might experience in life will be used for the same. His good and His glory.

CHAPTER 9:

UNVEILED

At the bottom on my face was my condition
Broken looking to Him my new position
My performance was never up to task
What liberation when finally taking off the mask

THE SCRIPTURE TEACHES US THAT THE LORD JESUS IS THE
same yesterday, today, and forever. He does not change. I needed
an awakening of sorts in my life. I needed to see that my only hope
was in Him who had saved me. Everything that can be shaken will
be shaken in this life. Whether that be in our physical, emotional,
or spiritual realms, the turbulent world that we live in will test
our faith. I am thankful to have the assurance that I can be secure
in God. It took me being in an awful condition to finally see real
change in my life. We can be sure that when we are shaken, God is
at work in us. Hebrews 12:25-29 reads, "*See that you do not refuse
Him who speaks. For if they did not escape who refused Him who spoke*

on earth, much more shall we not escape if we turn away from Him who speaks from heaven, whose voice then shook the earth; but now He has promised, saying, "Yet once more I shake not only the earth, but also heaven. Now this, "Yet once more," indicates the removal of those things that are being shaken, as of things that are made, that the things which cannot be shaken may remain. Therefore, since we are receiving a kingdom which cannot be shaken, let us have grace, by which we may serve God acceptably with reverence and godly fear. For our God is a consuming fire." There were things in my life that needed some shaking and some things that needed to be removed. When I found myself laying on my back, I was finally in a position to be saved.

Sunrise over the Temple Mount

The Temple Mount in Jerusalem is probably the most important piece of real estate in the world. At this place where Solomon's Temple once stood now stands a mosque. At the middle of every Middle East peace attempt, this small area of land plays a significant role. I had the opportunity to travel to Israel late in 2006 and visit this special place. It is most likely that very place where Abraham took Isaac up to be sacrificed, but was spared. It was also at that place where David bought the threshing floor and built an altar. Later, Solomon would build the Temple on the same site. Many years later, Jesus walked into that very temple and turned over the money changers' tables. And it will be at this same place where Jesus will enter again through the Eastern gate upon His Second Coming. During my time in Israel, I wanted to view this place from the Mount of Olives. This area of Jerusalem was not on our itinerary, so I woke up early one morning and called a cab. I had the cab driver take me to a hotel on the Mount of Olives overlooking the Temple Mount. It was a tremendous view of the entire Old City of Jerusalem. I stayed there for a couple of hours, watching the sunrise over that beautiful place. As the sun rose, as it had each day for thousands of years, the glory of its beauty was revealed. As I think about that special moment, I think of a new beginning and a new hope. Although that place is politically and religiously disputed today, it won't be long before the truth is unveiled. There will be an unmasking of all the fallacy in the world, as Jesus ushers in a new day.

When our faults and sins are unveiled and unmasked, we are then exposed to the healing that God desires for us. It is humiliating to have our sins exposed, but when they are, the sun begins to rise on us, and then His glorious plans can be revealed and carried out.

So thankful Mom was there

My dad served our country in the Vietnam War, but didn't really talk about it much. I would occasionally ask him things about his time there because I really wanted to know what he experienced. He was wounded in battle and was awarded the Purple Heart. I would sometimes get it out and look at it. Holding that medal in my hand represented something very significant in his life. And fortunately, he was there to tell me about it. He once told me the story about how he received the Purple Heart. His company was out on patrol traveling down a narrow road when gunfire suddenly broke out toward them. He was standing on the back of a tank when suddenly he was struck by a bullet in his left shoulder. When I asked him what it felt like, he said, "It felt like someone hit me with a sledge hammer." The blow of the impact threw him off the back of the tank. He said he laid on the ground, and the first thought that came to mind was, "I wish my mom was here." I am always touched when I think about what he said.

I was not hit by a bullet, but in my situation, I was certainly laying on my back feeling as if I had been. And just like my dad, in that moment, I wanted to be with my mom. Mom was gracious enough to leave her home in Texas to come and stay with me in Missouri. She and her dogs came and stayed with me. It was such a relief to have had her there during that very traumatic time. We spent a lot of time together during those weeks. Up until that point, our relationship had been very rocky. I can happily say that some of the first steps in my healing process were the conversations I had with mom. We talked a lot about our pasts and the struggles that our family had experienced. It was during those three weeks that I finally learned about my parents' divorce. I had always been upset at her, thinking that she had given up and quit on dad. But, I learned that she was not the one that had filed divorce papers. While I listened to her tell what had happened, my heart went out to her and we both cried a lot. It really didn't matter to me who had been at fault, it just helped to know what had happened. As I think about mom reading this at some point, I hope she knows I am proud to call her mom. It makes me happy to think back to those few weeks we were able to spend together. She was gracious and she was understanding. And that meant a lot to me.

Just like me, my parents made some mistakes. But you know what? I love them very much and am thankful for the efforts they both made to raise me and give me a good life. One thing is for sure. All three of us have learned that with Christ, we are forgiven! And praise God, we are all better Christians serving God today. Family problems can be so destructive if left to linger, simmer, and fester. If you have a family relationship that is strained and may need forgiveness, please take time right now and consider doing something about it. I would prayerfully ask you to consider approaching that family member in an effort to make things better. It is simply amazing what can happen. And it is incredible how relationships can blossom when the bondage of sin and unforgiveness are broken. When the bondage is broken, wonderful life will spring forth.

CAN ONE GET MUCH LOWER?

I suppose in reality I was just quite sick. My physical, emotional, and spiritual health were simply poor. My body-shape looked fine, but inside I was hurting. I had the outward appearance of health, but was really sick on the inside. And the root cause of this sickness was a deficiency in my spiritual diet. There was a lot of lukewarm activity going on in my life before our separation, but God wanted me to change that. Only by looking to him and getting the proper spiritual diet from His Word was that possible. Dr. Harry Kraus writes, "*Just as God designed our physical bodies to need specific nutrients for survival and fitness, so he has created us as spiritual beings to need balanced spiritual nutrition for fitness. Our physical bodies need amino acids, the building blocks of protein, carbohydrates for energy, essential fatty acids, vitamins, minerals, and plenty of water. Our spiritual food must come from feasting on Christ Himself, through a balanced consumption of every section of God's Word.*"

I like how Krauss uses the word feasting. I was nowhere near feasting. Rather, I was simply having a snack here and there.

I needed some shaking. When we understand the root of Sin and the Exchanged Life through the Life of Christ, we will consider the shaking of God in our lives as a blessing. Scripture tells us that we were all born into Adam (into a sin nature/life), but when we accept the work of the Cross of Christ, that sin nature is exchanged for a new nature. This new nature born of Christ is what Paul referred to in Galatians 2:20 when he says, *"it is no longer I that live but Christ that lives within me."* The process of God shaking us is a process to bring us to this understanding. I was so low at that time of my life. But because of His shaking, I could finally be healed.

WEARING THE MASK

People wear a lot of masks. I did too. Masks only serve to hide what is underneath. And when we wear a mask, it hides what is really happening inside and can only prolong our help and healing. If only I would have been exposed earlier. Then maybe some pain could have been averted. I Corinthians 13:12 says, *"For now we see in a mirror, dimly, but then face to face. Now I know in part, but then I shall know just as I also am known."* It felt so nice to finally have the mask off, because when our true identity is revealed, God can work through us. I believe the enemy uses masks in a lot of different ways, but they all have one thing in common. Masks are used to keep us from acknowledging who we really are. They are used to hinder the humility God wants us to exhibit. And masks serve to counter the confession and openness God desires for us in relation with Him.

Do not be deceived

When our focus is always on ourselves, we lose sight of His purposes and plans to help and save people around us. That was my problem. And when this selfishness sets in, we are ripe for deception. We can think we are so right, but be so far from the truth. I used to argue and debate people every chance I could get. But it was a terrible condition to live in. But regardless of where we have been, we can actually change into the new creation that God intends for us to be. In a world with so many counterfeits and misguided philosophies, we can still find hope and meaning. I am fully persuaded of that. In I Corinthians 15:31, the Apostle Paul said that "he dies daily." One can die to many things in the Christian walk in terms of wants, desires, and fleshly ambitions. But we also need to die to the idea that we deserve things. When I was finally broken and laying on my back, I realized that all I deserved was what God wanted for me. That was all and that was enough. I had to let go of my selfish ambitions and begin to seek His desires for my life. Dr. Krauss also writes, *"Self-deception is subtle and by nature isn't recognizable to the one being deceived. That frightens me. Sometimes only my spouse can see when my motives are tainted. At those times, my natural reaction is to defend myself rather than to humbly take off the pride-blinders that have given me such tunnel vision about an issue."*

Getting together on Friday nights

A couple weeks after my separation, one of the men from the church reached out to me. He invited me to a recovery group that met at the church every Friday night. We would have dinner at 6:00 and then would start our meetings at 7:00. There was always a time of singing and a lesson, but my favorite time would come last. At around 8:00, the women went into one room and the men stayed in another. This time was reserved for confidential confession and sharing about each other's lives. This was really the first time in my life that I had opened up to a group of people about the issues I was having. I can remember I was nervous that first night, but after that, I looked forward to it every week. The Bible talks about confessing our sin, and it is a powerful thing. I will always remember those Friday nights as one of the best times in my process of healing. As I think back to those precious meetings, I know that God was working in every person there. It takes a special courage to talk about one's problems with another person. But through that process there is a lifting of the veil. And when the veil is lifted and the mask is taken off, we can be seen for who we really are. If you are like I was, and are hiding some problem or sin in your life, I can only encourage you to find someone to talk to. It is such a relieving process to have that burden lifted that you have been carrying for so long. Jesus wants to lift us out of our sin. And one of the steps to make that happen, is for us to admit our problem, confess our problem, and then let Jesus heal us. Please don't do what I did by waiting too long. Instead, deal with your issue now. It will be painful at first, but the results will be good.

How many people know about this?

In the following weeks and months of my separation, I felt quite strange being in public places. There were so many crazy thoughts about what people might have thought about me. At times I actually found myself avoiding people. If I was approached by someone in a store and they asked how I was doing, I was never sure how to respond. I would often think, "Do they know what has happened? Do they know that my family is no longer together? It was a difficult time, but I received some good counsel from a friend of mine. Ken LaRue sent me an email on May 21, 2015 at 7:18 AM. Ken knew everything that had happened with me and was very encouraging. This message is even more special to me now, because Ken died not too long after this. Here is what he wrote:

"Hi Chris:

In my prayer time just now the Lord revealed some truth to me that I needed. Then I felt impressed to share it with you. As you know in Ephesians 1:13, our Spirit is sealed with His. Then in Ephesians 2:6, we are now seated in heaven with Him in our spirit. Now this is what He said to me, yes your spirit is sealed, and you are seated with me in the heavenly, but if you are to put on my likeness, you are to bring your soul to abide in my presence. Not visit, but dwell and abide in my presence."

What Ken told me, in that last email I would receive from him, is so true. We are to abide in the presence of the living God. Not just visit, but abide! And when we do that, we do not have to worry about what others are thinking. We will find ourselves in a state of peace and contentment in the presence of Christ. It takes an effort to withdraw and get alone with God, but what peace is to be found there. And the best example of this is what Jesus did himself. Luke 5:16 says, *"So He Himself often withdrew into the wilderness and prayed."*

LEARNING THROUGH MASSIVE TRAUMA

The process that God uses to heal us can sometimes be painful. Most people, by the time they reach the age of a young adult, are set in their ways. Their personality, temperament, and habits have most likely been firmly established. And although this is usually true, we don't have to stay stuck in our ways. We simply need to say, "Lord, please deliver me from myself."

Maybe if Congress were writing a new bill for our spiritual growth, it would be, "The Repeal of the Self-Preservation Act." I had a lot of self-preservation in my life. But when one is sick and tired of being sick and tired, they should turn to God. David Wilkerson writes, *"Yet, as we turn inward to examine our own spiritual condition, we're sickened by what we see there also. Finally, we cry out, "Lord, I've had enough of this backslidden, ineffectual Christianity. I want to be delivered from the power of sin and materialism. And I want a heart that's pure and holy before you. I refuse to just drift along in these last days, satisfied with a lukewarm spirit. I want to be a light for Jesus amid this wicked generation."*

God has given us a way out of our misery. It may be painful, but when we break free from the bondage that has held us, the joy is overwhelming. It is by His grace that we are saved. Behind that once untorn veil sat the Mercy Seat of God, where the High Priest would sprinkle the sacrificial blood once a year. But now, the Blood of Jesus has given us full access to His mercy and grace. Hugh Stowell wrote a hymn in 1828 about having peace at the Mercy Seat titled, "From Every Stormy Wind That Blows." David Levy, in his book The Tabernacle, writes, *"Two stanzas of the hymn sum*

up the fellowship that awaits each blood-bought believer who comes
to the mercy seat through Jesus Christ:

> From every stormy wind that blows,
> From every swelling tide of woes,
> There is a calm, a sure retreat
> 'Tis found beneath the mercy seat
> There is a place where Jesus sheds
> The oil of gladness on our heads;
> A place than all besides more sweet
> It is the blood-bought mercy seat

CHAPTER 10:

FULL EXPOSURE

The word was out, my sin exposed
No sense in hiding, everybody knows
Time alone with God is what I needed
The council of His word I heeded

EXPOSURES

When we are exposed, it shows what is really going on inside of us. When I think of being exposed, I think of photography. I really enjoy photography, and I guess if asked what is my hobby, that would be it. No one that I know of really wants to have their picture taken when they aren't looking good or when they are misbehaving. We seem to only want our good sides captured. I recently returned from a trip where I had taken over 400 digital photos that are stored on my camera's memory card. The memory card is about the size of a postage stamp and has the capacity to hold a couple thousand photos. I don't know about you, but that is mind boggling to me and the whole concept is hard for my limited mind to comprehend. It has only been recently that we have been able to experience and enter into this capacity of technological functions that God's physical elements and scientific laws have always held. These scientific possibilities have been inherent to the Creation since the beginning of time and the entire digital world that we are continuing to move into fascinates me.

The main reason it fascinates me is because it gives another look into the awesome power and creativity of God. I enjoy using my digital camera and am amazed how the image, or as I would like to call it, a "moment in time" can be captured in a molecular state and then transferred or transmitted by various methods if desired. To take digital photos and videos, and then to be able to transfer in that digital state is quite an engineering achievement. I wonder if we will ever be able to transfer digital smells? I do know this though – God spoke Creation into existence by His Word. And He said, "Let there be." The elements, the molecular structures, the physical laws – all of these things were set into existence by His voice and they have remained consistent and constant to this very day.

The potential was there from the beginning. Then, as scientists and engineers were given further revelation of the inherent characteristics of God's creation, we were extended more opportunities to enjoy it. Will we give credit where it is due? To deny the truth of this is to give credence to the statement written by Paul in Romans 1:22, "Professing themselves to be wise they became fools." A photo (file/record) can potentially be taken of any given subject during a split second of time from an almost infinite number of perspectives on an X,Y,Z coordinate system. Neither technology nor human efforts are capable of capturing a single moment from every possible perspective. But God can and has. And in computer terms, one might say that God has an infinite sized hard drive. It would also be safe to say that God "is memory" since He is all-seeing and all-knowing.

We know that the Lord is omnipresent by reading Psalm 139:7-12 and know that God sees everything as we read in Hebrews 4:13, "*And there is no creature hidden from His sight, but all things are naked and open to the eyes of Him to whom we must give account.*" If we believe this, it is easy to acknowledge God has a file (record) of you and I from every split second from every angle in every living moment we have ever experienced. You sometimes hear people say that God is never caught by surprise. One evangelist asked the question, "Has it ever occurred to you that nothing ever occurred to God?" What does the Bible have to say about it? The Lord has seen the end from the beginning, revealed by Isaiah 46:10 where we read, "Declaring the end from the beginning, and from ancient times the things that are not yet done, saying, My counsel shall stand, and I will do all my pleasure." And even further, we can recognize we will be held accountable for these "captured moments."

There is an extraordinary verse found in Revelation 20:12, "*And I saw the dead, small and great, stand before God; and the books were opened; and another book was opened, the book of life; and the dead were judged out of those things which were written in the books, according to their works.*" Just think how much computer memory it would take to store every file or image and sound from every split second in history at every angle for every person that ever lived! That would be quite the memory – but that is the mind of God! When you look around people's homes, most people display desirable photos. Although this is the case, there are also images of each of us in God's "album" we would not want displayed.

I am thankful we have a merciful and gracious Lord. Unfortunately, we all have some "digital files" in our past that are in the Lord's history book we would like to forget. But simply wanting them erased is not enough. The fact is, we must be reconciled back to God through the Blood of His Son, Jesus Christ. When we accept the work of Jesus, we can be assured of what we read in Hebrews 8:12, *"For I will be merciful to their unrighteousness, and their sins and their iniquities will I remember no more."* I would encourage you to embrace the work of the Cross and accept the Life of Christ from yours. Consider this, eternity depends on it. The next time you take a digital photo, give these things some thought. As for me, I hope my images in God's sight today are pleasing to Him. They haven't always been. But thanks to the work of God in my life, I don't have to shy away from the camera anymore.

FULL ACCESS

There are many exclusive places in the world, and I suppose the Oval Office in the White House would be one of them. Several years ago a friend and I had the opportunity to visit the Oval Office. We proceeded through the checkpoint with my friend Katie, after having our identification verified. I had met Katie a couple weeks earlier through an adoption client. She invited me back for a West Wing tour, so I took the opportunity. It was quite an experience. We toured two levels of the West Wing, the Cabinet Room, and the Press Briefing Room. We walked past the Security Briefing room but didn't go in. As we approached the Oval Office door and looked in at the President's desk, thoughts ran through my head of the many historical decisions that had been made in that room. I will have to admit that I got a little teary-eyed at the reality of standing there in that special place. As I think about that great day and getting to see the West Wing, my thoughts turn to what majesty and awe it will be to stand in the presence of the Lord at His Throne in Heaven. If a visit to the Oval Office brought such great emotion, it is hard to imagine the magnitude of worship we will experience before Christ Himself. Unlike the Oval Office, where I had to know someone of importance to get an invitation and where we had to go through security measures, our invitation to the Holy of Holies is open to anyone that accepts the free gift of Salvation. The time in my life after the separation was a time of loneliness, but was also a precious time to be alone with God. Painful? Yes. But beneficial? Absolutely! If you are alone at this time in your life, take this opportunity to spend time with your Creator in Heaven. You will find satisfaction and rest.

TIME WITH THE WORD OF GOD

What is your relationship with the Word of God? I realize that some people have never even held a Bible. For someone that has, perhaps, been around church all their life, that may come as a surprise. But many people have never picked up a Bible, let alone read it. And I suppose there are many church-goers that really don't give it much attention either. I would describe my former relationship with the Bible as mediocre at best. The Bible is key to unlocking a quality relationship with God as He speaks to us through it. It was during this time in my life where I learned to spend time alone with the Lord in His Word. Up until then it was such an on and off discipline. And because of that, my spiritual health suffered. Jimmy Evans writes, *"Chronically defeated believers also have a common thread. They have a convenient relationship with the Word of God. They are dating it but haven't decided whether to marry it or not. They have a cafeteria mentality as it relates to the Bible. They like to skip over the meaty parts and take the sweet parts. The result is chronic spiritual anemia."*

YIELDING TO THE KING OF KINGS

When we have been exposed and everyone knows our situation, it can feel a little uncomfortable. I used to walk through places feeling awkward, wondering what people were thinking about me. When we have been exposed, it is a humiliating process. I had been humiliated. But, that humiliation was a good thing. I think we often have a negative thought when it comes to the word humiliation, but it can be a positive thing. In my case, once my issues were exposed and out in the open, I was humbled to talk about it and get some help. If you are being humiliated, please know that some good can come from it. Jesus was humiliated. But, unlike me, He did not deserve it. His humiliation served to provide a way for each of us to be reconciled to God. His humiliation provided a path that we could follow. A path of righteousness and holiness. When I was in Israel, I stood outside the walls of Old Jerusalem and looked upon the place, believed to have been, where Jesus was Crucified. The way by which Jesus paid the price for our sin was quite incredible. People mocked him and ridiculed him. He was exposed on that Cross to die for us. Why the cross? John Stott writes, *"The Christians choice of a cross as the symbol of their faith is more surprising when we remember the horror with which crucifixion was regarded in the ancient world. The fact that a cross became the Christian symbol, and that Christians stubbornly refused, in spite of the ridicule, to discard it in favor of something less offensive, can have only one explanation. It means that the centrality of the cross originated in the mind of Jesus Himself."* When we are exposed, a wonderful humiliation can begin to take place. Jesus didn't need to be humiliated. He didn't deserve it. But, He was obedient and went to the Cross for us anyway!

SO MUCH ADVICE IN THE WORLD TODAY

The Lord didn't need my assistance to help his reputation, but I was concerned about the bad witness I had been. The last thing I wanted to do in life, was to be a bad example. There are so many philosophies and theories today. In fact, there always has been. In the midst of all of them, I had proclaimed the life changing impact of following Jesus. And the last thing I wanted to do was to be a blemish on my Christian faith. So I thank the Lord that He is in the forgiving and correcting business. He knew I would make these mistakes even before I was born and still loved me enough to save me. Billy Graham said, *"God loves you just like you are, but loves you too much to leave you that way."* So I had to go through a healing process. A painful, but gracious, healing process. Charles Spurgeon said, *"Experience teaches. This is the real school for God's children. I hardly think that we learn anything thoroughly without the rod of affliction. Certainly, we know best the things that have been a matter of personal experience. We need that truth to be burned into us with the hot iron of affliction before it can be of use to us.*" At that point in my life, after a long series of difficult events, I was personally experiencing the School of Christ that Spurgeon spoke of. If you are going through difficulties right now, take time to get on your knees before God and ask Him what He wants to teach you through it.

DAY TRIP TO THE TAJ MAHAL

We need time alone with God. It was a warm and humid morning as I walked outside of the hotel lobby in New Delhi. I had booked a day-trip from Delhi to Agra, to see the Taj Mahal. Near the half-way point of the four-hour drive, we stopped at a roadside café and break area. There were quite a few people there. Well, in India there are always a lot of people everywhere. And this was no different, with the exception of more tour buses full of people coming and going. After a short time getting something to eat and drink I headed back to the car and driver. I noticed a man standing in the middle of the parking lot. He looked to be a Westerner traveling just like I was. He was a relatively tall man and had graying hair and a mustache. With all the hustle bustle going on around him, he just stood there in the middle of that parking lot. He had his arms together behind his back and his feet were a little wider than shoulder width. With his eyes closed, and head tilted back, his face was looking squarely toward the sun. The sun was hot that day, but the warmth felt good. What impressed me about him was that he was enjoying the moment as if nothing else around him mattered. At that point in my life, I was never able to do that. To be able to stand still in quiet and take in the moment was a foreign concept to me. But I will never forget how that impressed me.

Now, I do the same thing. No matter where I go, I try to take a moment at some point to stop and stand still in the middle of whatever is going on. I then put my hands behind my back, and with eyes closed, stand squarely looking at the sun. Experiencing the energy of the sun on my face is a great time to appreciate the moment and reflect on the power of God. Try it some time. Stop where you are. Don't worry about who is looking, and simply take in the moment. Stand still and take in the energy of the physical sun and the Spiritual Son. We need time alone with God. If Jesus thought it was important to get alone and have personal quiet time in prayer with the Father, how much more so should we? Taking a brief moment to experience the power of the Sun and be still may not seem like a lot. But the ability to stand still and quiet before the Lord is a powerful thing. Take the opportunity and don't discount the benefit of resetting your perspectives.

THE UNAPOLOGETIC SCRIPTURE

If you would, please take time to read slowly through this next Scripture passage a couple times. Hebrews 4:12-13 says, *"For the word of God is living and powerful, and sharper than any two-edged sword, piercing even to the division of soul and spirit, and of joints and marrow, and is a discerner of the thoughts and intents of the hearts. And there is no creature hidden from His sight, but all things are naked and open to the eyes of Him to whom we must give account."* When we examine Scripture closely, we find that it examines us. These two verses make it quite clear that the Bible is not just some coffee table book filled with some interesting stories. No, it is the living Word of God Himself. The passage says that His Word is Living and it is Powerful. Let me ask you this ... Are the living words of God making a powerful impact in your life? If so, then you must be spending quality time with it. If not, I would kindly suggest that you make it a priority in your life. When the Word of God begins to examine us, we start to see our motives for what they are. We see more clearly why we might be the kind of person we are and why we desire certain things in life. The passage also tells us that no creature is hidden from His sight. Depending on your perspective, this can be a wonderful thing or a frightening thing. I have come to find when we are seeking God in a proper way, we embrace the changes He wants in our life. But when we, perhaps, only want God in a convenient sense, His sought-after changes in our life are not as inviting to us. It really speaks to the degree of selfishness in our life. The self-life can be a powerful thing. Just like weeds in our gardens, they have no trouble growing and taking over the good plants. Just like the weeds, our selfishness flourishes without any effort at all. Keeping a garden clean and fresh is well worth the good fruit it produces. Isn't our spiritual and mental fruit worth the time and effort it takes to cultivate? In our flesh, our selfishness is impossible to deal with on a long-term and consistent basis. But when we yield to His Word and let Jesus work, that selfishness starts to fade away. I needed time alone with God. And during that time in my life, the solitude provided a way for me to do that. I am thankful.

THE QUIET PLACE

God knew I needed temporary isolation
In that quiet place there was consecration
Seeking forgiveness I was found kneeling
Guilt and condemnation no more, but healing

HAVE I BURNED THE SHIPS?

The story is told of the Spanish explorer and conquistador, Hernando Cortez, who, in 1519, ordered his men to burn the ships. Looking at overwhelmingly incredible odds against victory over the Aztecs, he did an amazing thing. Instead of giving a retreat to return to sea, he ordered his men to scuttle the ships; leaving them no other options but to win or to die. The direction was very clear … everything was on the line. The option to be defeated was eliminated. They would conquer as heroes, or die. They were eventually victorious. When we have no place to go, we can accomplish fantastic things. When I read this story, a few questions ran through my mind. Chris, what are you putting your time, effort, and resources into? Are you still putting hope into earthly things that will fade away? Have I completely abandoned any hope that I can improve myself by my own fleshly strength? When we are in isolation with God, and have abandoned all the rescue ships in our life, we will finally be in the place where true transformation and victory can happen.

THE PRECIOUS TIME ALONE WITH GOD

Andrew Murray wrote, *"Nowhere can we get to know the holiness of God, and come under His influence and power, except in the inner chamber. It has been well said: "No man can expect to make progress in holiness who is not often and long alone with God."* When you are in the secret and holy place with God, it is an amazing feeling. The peace that one feels when alone with the Father is quite special indeed. Why is it so hard then to get alone with God? I think perhaps it is due to the multitude of distractions that try to pull us in every direction. It is so easy to sit down in front of the internet, or find the house needs cleaning, or working in the kitchen, or watching a program. The list goes on and on. Even as I sit here and write this, my mind is being pulled in several different directions. It shouldn't surprise me then that I also get distracted when I try to pray. I have found when I wake up early in the morning and spend time with the Lord, that the rest of my day goes so much better. It is as if the quiet time early in the mornings serves as fuel to get us through the day. I am not a morning person, so it is hard for me to do this. But when I do, I am always more peaceful and at rest. Contrast that to a day when I get up just in time to shower, put on my clothes, and rush out the door. Those days do not go as well. There is something special about time alone with God. Some people might say that is like needing a crutch. Yes it is! I need God. I need God everyday in order to live out the best day possible. If we want to make good progress in our daily spiritual walk, we must have time alone with God.

Murray also wrote, *"Do not strive in your own strength; cast yourself at the feet of the Lord Jesus, and wait upon Him in the sure confidence that He is with you, and works in you. Strive in prayer; let faith fill your heart – so will you be strong in the Lord, and in the power of His might."* Murray knew this from experience. He lived it on a daily basis. We have to quit striving to accomplish things of our own desires, and instead, follow God's desires that we learn through these times of prayer. Do you have a regular quiet time with God each day? If not, please consider making this a priority in your life. You will find that time you spend with God each day, will make the remaining hours even more peaceful and productive. Strive in prayer … and find the place where our greatest work is accomplished.

EATING DINNER ALONE

This may sound strange, but prior to my separation, I had never really sat down in a restaurant by myself and had a meal. It felt strange at first, but I eventually got used to it. And now, I actually find it enjoyable. There is something to be said for being alone. When you are alone, you can come and go as you please. There is certainly a freedom in being alone. But, I don't want to do this much longer. Even with all the advantages that solitude offers, in my opinion it does not outweigh the advantages of having a spouse. At the time of this writing, I have been living by myself for over 4 years and I think it is time to have some companionship again. God has brought a wonderful woman into my life and I look forward to seeing what the future holds. Eating dinner alone in that restaurant for the first time was a little scary for me, but I am thankful for the lessons I have learned along the way. I learned I had to be satisfied being with myself, in order to be truly satisfied spending time with someone else. The last four years served as a time that I could learn to be content in the moment and be content with myself. Because I have learned how to live life alone, I will now be a better husband to my future wife. That is what I always wanted. But I had to take the long hard road to get here.

GIVEN THE OPPORTUNITY TO DIE

I think it is an old Marines saying that says, "*Everyone wants to go to heaven, but nobody wants to die.*" Or another way of putting it might be, everyone wants the reward, but not many want to do the work to get it. But with every new day of our life, we have the opportunity to die. Why would I say that? Because we have the opportunity to die to our wants, and instead, start taking on God's wants and desires. Delayed gratification is hard. Most of us want things our way and we want them right now. But that is not usually how things happen. Certainly, when we are alone, we have the opportunity to die to our old life and take on new priorities. After my separation, and while spending time alone with God, I found myself asking these questions:

- Why am I doing what I am doing?
- What do I want in life?
- What does my best life look like?
- What would I accomplish if I could not fail?
- If time and money were not a concern, how would my life change?

As I took each one of these questions to the Lord in prayer, He began to work on my heart to show me that my story could be used to help others. So, here I sit, making my best attempt to write about the difficult things in my life and how God saved me through them. I never really considered myself much of a writer, as you can tell from my grammar, but I hope the message comes through anyway!

LAYING ON THE FLOOR WITH MY BIBLE

Even though my past relationship with God had a lot of ups and downs, there are certain memories that will last forever. I used to spend early mornings or late nights in our basement laying in front of a blue-flame propane heater. The heat would warm the carpet on the floor and I would simply lay there reading my Bible with a hot drink. I would flip through the pages and read different things I had marked and hi-lighted over the years. It was a fantastic time of being in the presence of God. It was times like those that were priceless. When I think of myself and so many others trying to find some peace and meaning, I have to go back to those memories. God has been reminding me lately that no matter what is going on in this world, there is a special quiet place where we can fellowship with Almighty God. When we are in that place, we are reminded that we are forgiven and there is no more condemnation. Do you have a special place in your home where you can get alone with God? A place of prayer that you can go to? In the mornings, I get out of bed and go straight to my knees. It isn't always a long period of time. But I kneel there and ask the Lord to carry me through the day. I tell the Lord that this day is His. In the quiet place with God is the most important destination we can ever go to. I am thankful God is always there waiting to talk with me.

But finding quiet time is not always easy. As I said before, there seems to be no end to the distractions. John Bunyan wrote, "*The difficulty that the heart has in the time of prayer! No one knows how many byways and back lanes the heart has in which to slip away from the presence of God. How much pride the heart has, if enabled with expressive language to pray to him!*" Bunyan is certainly correct, but we must persist and be disciplined to keep steering our minds back to the Him whom is our Sufficiency.

MY MIND WAS RACING

For the first several months of my separation, my mind would continually loop through all the things that had happened and what had been said … I said this … she said that … should I do this … should I do that … what will people think … what will happen to me … what about the children? There were so many thoughts racing through my head at once, I thought I would go crazy. My doctor prescribed some medication for depression and anxiety and asked me to take them for one year. So I did. I cannot say it helped me that much, but who knows what would have happened if I had not taken them. When we go through something traumatic, whatever that may be, our mind does a lot of funny things. At least mine did. And with all sincerity, I can say that by the grace of God I kept my sanity. It was my faith in the Lord Jesus that kept me going each day. I would often get to work and just try to make it through the day. I guess I was being productive, but didn't always feel like it. Sometimes I would just put my head on my desk and try to block out the mental noise. Sometimes I would go into the bathroom and have a good cry. But somehow I kept going. I had a calendar that I would number the days that had passed since the separation. I documented everything that I could think of and tried to keep a journal. At this point, I was sure that we would be back together before long. Every day, I would get the calendar out and write down how many days we had been apart. At some point I started seeing a counselor and he told me I would eventually stop counting the days. Of course, I didn't believe him at the time. But he was right, and eventually I stopped counting … somewhere around 171 days :)

But what always helped me was my prayer time. The more I would pray the better I would feel. So I kept doing it, and eventually I started to feel 'normal' again.

CONSISTENT SUPPORT

Ultimately, I learned I could only depend on God. And really, wasn't that the whole point I was being taught? Yes, it was. And it became clearer and clearer as time went on. Do not get me wrong, I had family, friends, and a support network that was helping me. But they could not always be there. Everyone is busy, and let's be honest, people cannot carry us through our problems. Yes, God may use each of us to help another in times of need, but we must learn to seek God above everyone and everything else. Dave Carder writes, "*They can stand with you for a while, but the hard work you will often do by yourself in the middle of the night without a lot of support, except for the Son of Man who has gone through it before you.*" It was during those long nights, being alone with God, that I would cry out to Him for help and comfort. It is hard work to spend time alone with God when we are hurting. But we have to keep showing up. We have to keep going to the source of healing. A person once asked why another person wasn't at church. The other person replied, they were too sick to attend the healing meeting. Just a little humor, but when we are sick physically or mentally, we have to get to the healing place. And that healing place is in the presence of God.

RUNNING FAST, GETTING NOWHERE

One of my friends wrote an article once, titled *Running Fast, Getting Nowhere.* In the article he described the long laundry list of things that keep us busy each day and how it seemed like being on a hamster wheel. Bill would sometimes joke that he was in a rat race, and the rats were winning! The rats never seemed to get tired, but kept running and running in circles. A life lived without the precious quiet time in prayer, is like a life on the hamster wheel. Running and running, but never getting anywhere. What miraculous and powerful work we can accomplish when we stay in the quiet place of prayer. And in my situation, I was getting a chance to do just that. I praise God, I turned to him in thanks as He took me through the healing process. I could have turned in anger and ran from God, but He was gracious to me.

IT IS FINISHED

I believe that most religious activities are vain attempts to cleanse one from sin while a Life in Christ actually accomplishes it. When we acknowledge our sin, we begin the process of true recovery. We can go through all kinds of step programs and self-help methods, but unless a true confession and repentance of sin is involved, it will be in vain. We read a remarkable thing in Psalm 38:18, *"For I will declare mine iniquity; I will be sorry for my sin."* What an amazing verse this is! Can you imagine what would happen in our world if more people would simply be sorry for their sin. The Bible says that Jesus wept over Jersualem as he looked upon the people's worldly ways and their unforgiving and unbelieving hard-hearts. When the precious work of Christ becomes real to us, then we begin to truly see how bad our sin really is. A white sheep's wool may look white, but when standing in front of a pure-white background, the wool looks hideously dark and dingy. That is the same way with us. We may have the appearance of goodness and purity, but when we stand against the Holiness of God, every sin and blemish becomes noticeable. In my place of temporary isolation, I found myself standing in front of that Holiness, and the nasty stuff in my life came to light. Let each of us be sorry for the sin in our life. Truly sorry. When we are, the forgiveness that is there, will become manifested in us, bringing about wonderful changes in our thoughts and actions.

KNOWING THAT HE IS ENOUGH!

We need to be holding onto things very lightly. When we have someone or something that we are so dependent on, we are ripe to fail. I believe I had a lot of co-dependency in my life. I was so dependent on the love and approval of others that when they weren't there to prop me up, I felt inadequate and fearful. I learned that God had to be enough. No matter how important other things seemed to be, God had to be enough in my life. Up until that point, I had put my wife and family over God. It was really a form of idolatry. And God can simply not tolerate that. There is an interesting dialogue in the movie *Cool Runnings* with John Candy. Candy and the Jamaican Bobsled captain are sitting in their hotel having a conversation about what is really important.

Coach Irv: *Derice, a gold medal is a wonderful thing, But if you're not enough without one, you'll never be enough with one.* Derice Bannock: *Hey coach, how will I know if I'm enough?* Coach Irv: *When you cross that finish line tomorrow, you'll know.* In the movie, Bannock had come to learn that he was a complete person, even without an Olympic gold medal. The medal would have been nice, but in the end, he realized his true worth as a person. In my life, I had to understand that I was complete alone, if I had God. But if I was trying to find my value and worth in anyone or anything else, then I would fail. I am so thankful God taught me this.

THE HEALING I NEEDED

The quiet place is a sacred place. And it was in this place where I found healing. If you are reading this and you are still struggling with internal heart healing, please turn to the Lord in prayer. Seek

His face and know He loves you. I love the following quote by Jim Cymbala. Cymbala writes, *"Everything we will ever do or will ever be must come from God, and it comes the same way we started our spiritual walk. In other words, having started with a powerful work of God in our souls, are we now going to live for him on "I promise" power? No, our human effort is totally inadequate from the task. We need the water of the Spirit. God, who began the work in us, must continue it himself."* I believe this!

CHAPTER 12:

COSTLY GRACE

Truly repentant of choices in my soul
Looking to Jesus only to make me whole
Although many regrets and much time lost
Jesus has forgiven at a precious cost

WHEN I WAS A YOUNG BOY, A NEIGHBOR AND I HAD BEEN
playing in a nearby construction site where they were burning trash.
We poked around in it and had a good time. But, about an hour
later, we were playing in our backyard when we heard fire trucks
heading toward our subdivision. They passed our house and headed
to the construction lot with the fire. Apparently, in our efforts
to kindle the fire, the field had caught fire and several acres were
burning. Scared, we ran home and immediately told our parents
we didn't know anything about it. Several nights passed, and each
night I laid in my bed so convicted by the lie I had told them. The
agony over what I had done eventually was so miserable I had to

confess. One night, mom came into my room to pray with me. I could not stand it any longer, and with tears running down my face, told her what we had done. It was so difficult to do, but once I confessed my sin, what a relief I felt. It was an overwhelming release from the bondage of holding in that story. That night I finally confessed, was a night where true repentance happened. When we make a mistake, or intentionally do something wrong, we have to examine our hearts to see if true sorrow and repentance are there. But what a relief it is when we can finally accept the forgiveness that Jesus purchased for us by admitting our sin. We make a lot of choices in our lives, and some of them are not very good. But when we do, we have to ask ourselves if we are sorry.

YACHTS AROUND CAPRI

Beautiful things are often very costly. It is often the time and resources that have gone into something that makes it so valuable. It was a beautiful day as we hurried out of the train station to get a cab for the Naples Port. I had bought tickets for the ferry and we didn't have a lot of time to spare. There was a lot of activity around the port that morning, but we were able to make our scheduled departure for Capri. After nearly an hour on the ferry, we reached the Italian island where we saw many beautiful homes along the coast line and wonderful yachts anchored offshore. While on the island for three days, mom and I took several walks along the narrow streets, and were amazed at the beautiful and fascinating homes and buildings. What a cost these people must have paid to have afforded such exquisite homes. Not only were their homes beautiful, but the surrounding gardens looked amazing in their design and care. If we look at something in the material world such as a house, and can appreciate the cost it took to build, should we not also consider the cost of spiritual and emotional things as well? I believe we should, and even more so. My life had been in a mess. The ongoing cycle of fear, control, and anger did much to hurt myself and others. It was costly. The emotional problems that I had suffered through, did not go away by themselves. What I thought would be a quick fix to my problems, ended up taking several years. The process God takes us through will often be costly. But, the costly grace that God shows us through His Son Jesus accomplishes the healing we need. I was amazed by the extravagant and beautiful homes on Capri, but I am even more amazed at the work Christ performed for me. It was not cheap grace, but it was costly. A costly grace that Jesus gave His life for.

GETTING DISTRACTED WITH INSIGNIFICANT THINGS

Even though life is serious, and I know I am to keep my focus on eternal things, I still get distracted. I am ashamed to say I used to get caught up in so many petty arguments. I think I just liked to argue. At least that is what a few of my childhood teachers told me. There was something about standing up for what I believed in that I really liked. And don't get me wrong, I still stand up for my convictions. But now, I go about it in such a better way. When we react to disappointment or a difference in opinion with humility, God is pleased. It is the humility of Christ within us that helps us to navigate all the confusion and frustration around us. As we become closer to Jesus, our humility should be increasing. If pride is on the rise, then we should take a close examination of our walk with God. If our mind is veering away from what matters, then we open ourselves up to all kinds of fallacies. 2 Corinthians 4:18 says, *"while we do not look at the things which are seen, but at the things which are not seen. For the things which are seen are temporary, but the things which are not seen are eternal."* Paul, in his second letter to the Corinthian people, is telling them, in no uncertain terms, we are to keep our minds fixed on eternal things. In other words, instead of getting caught up in every argument or folly, we should stay focused on things of God. This is really hard for me. My mind gets pulled in so many directions. Even as I sit here and try to write, my mind continually jumps to other things. It takes a concerted effort and a certain degree of discipline to keep bringing our minds back to what the Word of God says. And if we believe that exercise helps our muscles, then we can certainly agree that the exercise of daily Bible time and prayer will condition us. We need to be conditioned to continually bring our thoughts back to what God says, and not what our emotions might be saying to us. I John 2:15 says, *"Do not love the world or the things in the world. If anyone loves the world, the love of the Father is not in him."* I hope you would agree with me that we should be loving God more than things the world can offer us. Ask the Lord to give you clarity and focus in your daily devotion and time with Him.

How much is your life really worth?

There is such fierce rage, arguments, and debates taking place in our society about abortion and women's rights. I have always found it amazing that some don't seem to have a problem taking a baby's life. This is simply unimaginable to me. But for some reason, others come to a different conclusion. How can this be? The mind can be deceived. Even I must acknowledge there are things I believe that could be wrong. It reminds me of a story about a minister who was traveling on an airplane. He was seated next to a man, whom through a mid-flight discussion, discovered was an atheist. He asked the self-proclaimed atheist, "Do you know everything?" And the man responded, "Of course not!" Then he asked the atheist, "Do you know even half of everything?" The man then responded, "Probably not." Then the minister said, "Well, even if you knew half of everything, what if God existed in the other half you don't know about?!" The example goes to show that we can be wrong about some things because of our limited knowledge, but for me, I believe we can find the answer to life in the Bible. And in the Scripture we are told that God knows us in the womb and even before we are created. So to think of taking an innocent life, is simply unimaginable. Let's pray for those still blinded by this awful travesty chalked up to "rights." I have always been a pro-life person, but had never really asked myself what my life was worth. When one considers all the impact they have on others, they see their lives are quite valuable.

LOVE ALL PEOPLE THE SAME

There are a lot of anti-discrimination laws in our society. It is a real shame it has to be that way. I suppose it is really an indictment of the selfishness of people. Or maybe it could be put this way. Discrimination of other people is really an expression of the pride and arrogance so many are caught up in. I had the opportunity to visit Selma, Alabama several years again. I walked over the Pettus Bridge where the Civil Rights activists had walked. When God is at the center of people's lives, people will be filled with his love. What a sad time for our nation to have endured. There was so much violence and hate in those days. And of course, there are still people that discriminate. But, by and large, I believe all people have an opportunity to succeed in our society. And now, those that still discriminate, are no longer respected. We do not have to believe like everyone else, and we do not have to condone all behaviors as equal. But we do need to love people and treat them with respect, regardless of their persuasions and affiliations. I am a believer in marriage between one man and one woman. I am a believer of the sanctity of life in the mother's womb. I am a believer of Jesus Christ, the risen Son of God, that is the sole mediator between God and man. But for those that may disagree with my positions, I can still love them. Why? Because God loves them. God will love people through us as we show them the costly grace that makes salvation possible. If we do not love people as God loves them, how will they ever know who He really is? God will use you and I to do his work as we submit ourselves unto Him in humility. But what if that person doesn't like me? Or what if that person ridicules me? Or what if that person discriminates against me? If we are in right relationship with Jesus, we will be found loving them anyway.

It is my opinion that everyone falls into one of two groups. Those that do not know Christ and those that have accepted the work of Christ, but still need a deeper relationship with Him. So I pray these words will compel you to seek the Lord with all your heart, mind, soul, and strength.

God loves us, but hates our sin

God's love toward us is not permission to sin. We cannot take the gracious love of God as a liberty to live a life in opposition to His Word. Regardless of what kind of trouble or sin we find ourselves in, we have to know that God loves us. He loves us, but doesn't want us to stay the way we are. When we realize what price was paid for the forgiveness of our sin, we reckon the true cost of grace. Dietrich Bonhoeffer wrote, *"Costly grace is the hidden treasure in the field, for the sake of which people go and sell with joy everything they have. It is the costly pearl, for whose price the merchant sells all that he has; it is Christ's sovereignty; for the sake of which you tear out an eye if it causes you to stumble. It is the call of Jesus Christ which causes a disciple to leave his nets and follow him."* I don't know about you, but what Bonhoeffer wrote does not sound like a casual relationship with God. It sounds like commitment. It sounds serious. It sounds like something worthy of our praise and adoration. Yes, the costly grace of Christ is not to be taken lightly. We can be joyful knowing that a full surrender to His purpose and His way will make us a success. There is the account of the Samaritan woman at the well in John chapter 4. Jesus told her that she was to go and sin no more. Yes, her sin would be forgiven, but she was now told to turn and sin no more. The grace of Jesus not only saves us, but it also keeps us from sin. The grace of God works through us to purge out those sin areas of our life. The grace of God is like clean water running through a sponge to remove the dirt and all the nasty things. For me, I knew that God loved me, but I also knew He didn't want me to continue down the path I was on. The costly and precious grace of Christ saved me and the costly grace of Christ also put me on a path of healing. I am thankful.

With that being said, we should be careful not to fall into the cheap grace trap. It is easy to fall into this. We want to get along. We don't want to hurt anyone's feelings. We don't want to rock the boat. Yes, of course we want to get along with people, but will still are commanded to preach the whole truth of Scripture. But with so much stress and temptation in life, we are tempted to take the easy way. So, a word of caution should go out to the proclaimers of a feel-good gospel that denies the holiness and righteousness of God. Bonhoeffer also wrote, *"Cheap grace is preaching forgiveness without repentance; it is baptism without discipline of community; it is the Lord's Supper without confession of sin; it is absolution without personal confession. Cheap grace is grace without discipleship, grace without the cross, grace without the living, incarnate Jesus Christ."*

COSTLY GRACE IN WESTERN KENYA

It was a dusty ride across the Rift Valley in East Africa. Our driver, Richard, was taking us to western Kenya to visit some friends over an Easter weekend. While living in a subdivision of Nairobi, not too far from the Kibera Slums, we met a special lady named Margaret. Margaret would go to the market each day and buy fresh Tilapia that had been caught in Lake Victoria the previous day. Each day, trucks would bring the fish from western Kenya into the markets of Nairobi. Margaret would buy a basket full of fish each morning and then carry her basket throughout the neighborhoods. We were fortunate enough to live in one of those neighborhoods on her route. She would sit in the driveway and fillet as many fish as we wanted to buy. It was something we could not do all the time, but the fresh fish was quite a treat when we did. But better than the fish, was the relationship that was formed with our families. We got to know her, and her son Daniel, quite well. So on the Easter weekend of 2010 we traveled to their home in western Kenya for a visit.

After the six hour drive, we were greeted at her home by many children playing soccer and several neighbors that had joined her family to welcome us. Margaret and her family were quite gracious. Their home was very simple, but we felt comfortable and at ease with them. They made a tremendous meal for us, and after dinner, we sang worship songs in the main room of the house. After we sang for about an hour, the sun started to go down. Being without electricity, Margaret lit several oil-burning lamps, and we started a short Bible-study. It was such a fantastic moment in time. One that I will never forget. There we were in a small mud and stick-built home having a Bible study under the oil lamps with Kenyan people of various tribes. The presence of the Lord was there and everyone knew it was a special night. There is unity at a time like that where no color, status, or tribe can disturb. Margaret's home was filled with the peace of God that night. It was the costly Grace of Christ that had saved her. It was the costly Grace of Christ that had saved our driver Richard. It was the costly Grace of Christ that had saved us. And for that night, we all experienced that Grace of Christ as He anointed the singing and Bible study. I am thankful for that night in western Kenya.

REPENTANCE WILL EQUAL CHANGE

Repent and you shall be saved. This is what the Bible teaches us. Can we be saved with some cheap grace of just going through the religious motions? We cannot. And one should stay clear of any teaching that says otherwise. True salvation happens when we come to the knowledge of our sin and then turn in true repentance from it. True salvation will reveal Jesus to us in a way that shows His omnipotent power, and not simply relegate Him down to some other teacher or prophet. Graeme Goldsworthy writes, *"A preaching dealing with the actual sayings of Jesus will find it too easy to slip into the error of conveying the idea that the essence of Christianity is what Jesus taught. People will soon reduce the notion of the teachings of Jesus to a few ethical generalities or the golden rule. Jesus is left as merely the good teacher. Let the preacher who would preach on the parables of Jesus take heed!"* Jesus told us He Himself was the I AM. The I AM has spoken and we need to value His grace as a priceless gift. This Man was crucified for me and I will worship Him! Philippians 2:9-11 says, *"Therefore God also has highly exalted Him and given Him the name which is above every name, that at the name of Jesus every knee should bow, of those in heaven, and of those on earth, and of those under the earth, and that every tongue should confess that Jesus Christ is Lord, to the glory of God the Father."* Amen!

CHAPTER 13:

SING PRAISES

Opportunity gone by, feeling deep sorrow
The Lord forgives and brings a new tomorrow
The pain of the past went for so long
But now I gloriously sing a new song

THE BURDEN OF REGRET

No matter what our past issues have been, we will most likely feel some regret. Although things are good now, when I look back at all the years I struggled, there is some regret. There is a certain amount of emotional baggage until God cuts us free from the guilt and pain. I laughed upon seeing a cartoon recently where a man is standing at the check-in counter at the airport. The lady behind the counter said, "*Yes sir, the charges are correct. We now charge for emotional baggage.*" I thought that was pretty funny, but it is also true. Emotional baggage costs us so much when it takes away from the freedom and liberty God desires us to have. The issue for most people is that they don't know how to free themselves from it.

There is an interesting sequence of scenes in the movie *The Mission* with Robert DeNiro. At some point in the movie, he is given a punishment and is required to haul a huge and very heavy cargo bag up the side of a cliff. The bag is connected to a rope over his back. It is an agonizing and very difficult burden to carry. The burden that he is required to lift and carry up the side of the mountain looks nearly impossible, but somehow, he makes it to the top. Just before he gets to the top, one of the native people takes out a knife and cuts the rope. The cargo is left to fall to the bottom of the cliff and he is set free. What a tremendous picture of what it is like for us to carry the burden of sin and guilt. It is difficult. It is dangerous. And if we are not set free, it can kill us. The Bible says the wages of sin is death. And that death can come in two parts. First, it certainly kills us in a spiritual sense, but it can also result in a physical death.

I am thankful to have been set free from the bondage that kept me captive for so many years. But I could have never accomplished that freedom in my own strength. I could improve myself for a short period of time, but eventually, I would fall right back into the same old habits and behavior. This was so frustrating. It is a terrible feeling to want to be free, but finding yourself unable to get there. Dietrich Bonhoeffer wrote, "*People can shake off the burdens laid on them. But doing so does not free them at all from their burdens. Instead, it loads them with a heavier, more unbearable burden. They bear the self-chosen yoke of their own selves.*" It was Bonhoeffer, before he was executed by the Nazis in World War II, that described the costly grace and cheap grace in his book on discipleship. He also understood the bondages that men faced and were held captive by. But the other people he described were those that fell into the grace of God and were set free from their bondage.

THE OPPORTUNITY NOW

Is change really possible? Is it possible for someone that has lived a certain way most of their life? Does that person have a hope? You need to realize as you read these words that change is possible. Is does not matter what you feel in your emotions. Well, it does matter of course. But, what you feel in your emotions should not supersede what God says is true. If the Lord says that he can makes all things new, then certainly you can take on a new life. The Apostle Paul was a radical character in the Jewish faith. He was committed to his cause and was among the best in education and obedience to the Law. But there came a day when Jesus revealed Himself to Paul. Paul went through a miraculous transformation, and then spent the rest of his life preaching and proclaiming the Good News of Salvation. It doesn't matter how bad your life has been, or what your current issues may be, God wants to change you.

The Lord God called out to the prophet Jeremiah and said this, "*Call to Me, and I will answer you, and show you great and mighty things, which you do not know.*" Jeremiah 33:3 The fact is, we can simply be ignorant of things. This is not a derogatory statement, but rather, it just means we don't know what we don't know. As you read this, you may be unaware that change is really possible. For me, trying to overcome my struggles of control and anger seemed impossible. But when my life was shaken in a traumatic way, I called out to God, and he began the healing process in me. Because of this, I am joyful. I am thankful. And I can now look back on past regrets with grace, knowing the days ahead are so much better. I am not sure if all of the pain and regret will ever go away. But the difference now is those thoughts don't consume me. They are fleeting thoughts that are quickly taken away by the realization of who I am today. Yes, there is opportunity today. There is an opportunity for you to see a change, and realize you can be made whole again.

Humpty Dumpty can be put back together

You are probably familiar with Humpty Dumpty, the old nursery rhyme riddle. The earliest known version, published in Samuel Arnold's *Juvenille Amusements* in 1797, provides a vivid and appropriate illustration for us as frail and damaged human souls.

> Humpty Dumpty sat on a wall,
>
> Humpty Dumpty had a great fall.
>
> All the King's horses and all the king's men
>
> Couldn't put Humpty together again.

Although Humpty, in the original versions, may not have been an egg-shaped character, the egg is what comes to most people's minds today. I was impressed when listening to a sermon by Evangelist and teacher, Gaylon Vinson, as he preached on the regenerative power of God. Vinson used the illustration in such clear terms as to leave the listener with no doubt their lives could be put back together. Unlike Humpty, where there were so many unrepairable pieces, God can indeed put us back together. When the Lord heals us, all those broken pieces, that seemed impossible to put together, are healed. Will there be some scars and visible cracks? Yes, perhaps, and probably very likely. Sometimes families split. Sometimes relationships are torn apart. And in that sense, some of us will never be put back together like we were, but we will be whole again. We will be whole again in the Lord Jesus. The physical and worldly aspect of our lives may change, but the spiritual and emotional components of our being will be new. God tells us in His Word that we can be new creations in Him. That is the whole point. Humpty Dumpty could not be put back together, but we can be. Praise the Lord Jesus for the work He has done for us.

WHAT APPEARS TO BE RIGHT AND WHAT IS RIGHT

Watchman Nee, a Chinese Christian minister who was imprisoned for his preaching, never lost sight of the Truth of God's Word. Before he died in that prison, he continued to worship God and never lost his faith. Nee wrote a vivid illustration that comes to mind when I think about keeping my focus. Some might say we may reach a point of no return, where healing cannot happen. But that is simply not true. Nee wrote, "*You probably know the illustration of Fact, Faith, and Experience walking along the top of a wall. Fact walked steadily on, turning neither to right nor left and never looking behind. Faith followed, and all went well so long as he kept his eyes focused upon Fact; but as soon as he became concerned about Experience and turned to see how he was getting on, he lost his balance and tumbled off the wall, and poor old Experience fell down after him.*" Read through this a few times and think about your own life. Do you keep looking around at everything in order to determine your condition in life? Or do you keep your mind fixed on the Fact of

God's Word and what he says about you? During the process of my healing, it was great to meet with people in our men's small groups. To be in group of men that would openly discuss their past sins and confess their current issues was a blessing. I am happy to say, no one was ever condemning in those meetings. But rather, we continually reminded each other of the Fact. The Fact that God was in the healing business and our lives were made new by him. There was one gentleman that kept falling back into his old ways, but each week, we would receive him with open arms in love. It was the love of God that eventually made him whole again. Watchman Nee understood that as long as we keep our minds fixed on the Fact of God's Word, we will steadily walk on that wall of victory. But when we start looking around at our old experience, then we are subject to fall off again. By faith, we can resist that temptation to look around at all the negative and seducing thoughts, and continue walking in victory with the Lord God.

THE MAGNITUDE OF THE MOMENT

When I arrived home that Friday afternoon, and found my house empty, I wondered why it had to be so hard. God chose to do it His way. If left up to me, I would probably still be in a miserable rut. But God chose to act quickly, and in a sharp act of separation, He got my attention. A.W. Tozer wrote about the challenge that Abraham, that faithful man of God, faced as he was instructed to be obedient in a difficult situation we could only imagine. Tozer wrote, *"The old man of God lifted his head to respond to the Voice, and stood there on the mount strong and pure and grand, a man marked out by the Lord for special treatment, a friend and favorite of the Most High.*

Now he was a man wholly surrendered, a man utterly obedient, a man who possessed nothing. He had concentrated his all in the person of his dear son, and God had taken it from him. God could have begun out on the margin of Abraham's life and worked inward to the center; He chose rather to cut quickly to the heart and have it over in one sharp act of separation. In dealing thus He practiced an economy of means and time. It hurt cruelly, but it was effective."

GLORY HERE AND THERE

There are some events in life that hit the nerve of the soul in such a remarkable way that they leave an indelible memory on our minds. Moments like this are not just about the specific event, but rather, can speak to or relate to a connection with a higher purpose or calling. Special and significant events can be indicators of good or glory to come. And in light of Scripture, I see these special events as insights to the glory of God we will experience once face to face with Him. These earthly events can never come close to the magnitude of being in God's presence, but they give us a glimpse into the power and awe that awaits us. On Sunday, May 29, 2016, I sat in the grandstands at the 100th running of the Indianapolis 500. The sky was clear that day and the energy around the Speedway was absolutely incredible. Prior to the race that day, the announcer turned everyone's attention to the starting line where several Pearl Harbor veterans were seated. Honoring our veterans on that Memorial Day weekend was incredibly special. A moment of silence was observed, and the record crowd of 350,000 people were silent. I will never forget the magnitude of that moment. Shortly after that, the command was given, "Drivers start your engines!" With that, those same 350,000 people erupted into tremendous cheers. It brought tears to my eyes. What a moment to have experienced! The size of the crowd, the significance of the veterans, the technology of those fascinating racecars, the endurance of the drivers, and the sheer noise and energy of the Speedway. The combination of these things being brought together, was in a sense a glorious and powerful thing. I believe it is impossible for our human minds to fully comprehend the glory of God when we are inundated with so much interference and noise. But there are times, whether it be in an intimate quiet time of prayer or at an event of such magnitude, when we get a brief glimpse of His glory. What a day it will be, when His glory we will see. When God sets us free from the bondage we are in, it is a glorious day, and the heavens rejoice with us.

ANGELS AROUND THE THRONE

I enjoy reading through the Book of Revelation. I do not claim to understand all of it, but by reading it, I am given fascinating insights into the heavenly realm and things to come in our world. We see the majesty and power of God. And we are given glimpses into the real and very significant spiritual world around us. One of my favorite passages is in chapter 5. Revelation 5:8-14 says, *"And when he had taken the book, the four beasts and four and twenty elders fell down before the Lamb, having every one of them harps, and golden vials full of odours, which are the prayers of saints. And they sung a new song, saying, Thou art worthy to take the book, and to open the seals thereof: for thou wast slain, and hast redeemed us to God by thy blood out of every kindred, and tongue, and people, and nation; And hast made us unto our God kings and priests: and we shall reign on the earth. And I beheld, and I heard the voice of many angels round about the throne and the beasts and the elders: and the number of them was ten thousand times ten thousand, and thousands of thousands; Saying with a loud voice, Worthy is the Lamb that was slain to receive power, and riches, and wisdom, and strength, and honour, and glory, and blessing. And every creature which is in heaven, and on the earth, and under the earth, and such as are in the sea, and all that are in them, heard I saying, Blessing, and honour, and glory, and power, be unto him that sitteth upon the throne, and unto the Lamb for ever and ever. And the four beasts said, Amen. And the four and twenty elders fell down and worshipped him that liveth for ever and ever."* Worthy is the Lamb of God!

YOU ARE SPECIAL ... GOD HAS A PURPOSE FOR YOU!

I used to get letters from a pastor friend, and he would often include the words, "You are special." There was something very comforting about those words, and now I use them often as I communicate with other people. The fact is that we are special. And when we realize what our life is worth to God, it becomes more and more clear. When I think about the process required to adopt a child, it reminds me of how special life really is. People can debate about what constitutes a necessary adoption process, but in its present form, it can be challenging. But the challenge is worth it because a human life is involved. There are a lot of people trying to figure out what their purpose is. For now, part of mine is sharing this message. But this message is only a part of a larger plan to show people what a life in Christ can look like. Regardless of how

God uses each one of us, He sees us as His special son or daughter. When we realize how much God loves us and cares for us, we will then start resting in Him. Resting in God does not mean laying around doing nothing. No, but it means we are at peace and rest while we work each day in whatever capacity He has us. Hebrews 4:10 says, "*For he who has entered His rest has himself also ceased from his works as God did from His.*"

CHAPTER 14:

DEBACLE TO DELIGHT

Because of issues I was rightly faulted
Now through magnificent Grace, Christ is exalted
Devastating debacle to Divine delight
Fear no longer overcomes to indict

THE LOST LANGUAGE OF LAMENT

Michael Card has written a wonderful book, titled *A Sacred Sorrow*, that goes into great detail about the lost language of lament. In it, he shows several people from the Bible that went through great trials, and then lamented in sorrow because of their sin. In the book he also describes scenarios that we may be familiar with. One, for example, relates to the way we try to comfort people. Card very poignantly explains that when people are sorrowful over their sin, we should not try to pull them out of their sadness. That may sound strange, but his point is well taken. When a person is truly convinced of their sin problem, and as a result, finds themselves weeping over it in sorrow, we should not try to circumvent the process. It is often our natural human response to go up to that person, put our arms around them, and try to make them happy or smile. And while that is fine to a point, maybe what we should do is grieve with them. I believe it can be difficult to watch someone grieve. But that is part of the healing process and we should let God work through it in its entirety. When we try to rush the healing process by eliminating the grieving stage, we only prolong the full and true healing intended. Instead of trying to make someone happy in their grief, we should applaud them in their sincerity and honesty toward repentance. For me, I had to come to a place in my life where I was truly repentant of my fear. A place where I was truly repentant of my controlling behavior. And a place where I was truly repentant of my anger and outbursts. When that true repentance happened, there was grief. A person will grieve when they come to a full realization of what that sin meant and produced in their life. So for me, a grieving process followed. However, that painful and necessary process was for my good.

THE GREATEST RESCUE

We drove up to the airport terminal in Entebbe, Uganda and looked at the gunfire holes in the old traffic-control tower. One of the Africa Inland Mission pilots had picked us up from the airport after our flight from Nairobi. I told him I really wanted to see the old terminal, so he drove us over. Those holes I looked at now stand testimony to the successful Israeli rescue mission of 1976. The nation of Israel has had a lot of miracles in its history, and this rescue mission was certainly one of them. Operation Thunderbolt was planned after 106 people were held hostage by Idi Amin's rebel army, after an Air France flight traveling from Athens to Tel Aviv had been hi-jacked by members of the Popular Front for the Liberation of Palestine. It is regarded as one of the most spectacular secret military rescue missions of all time, if not the greatest. What the Israeli military pulled-off was nothing short of a miracle. To have flown all the way from Israel to Kenya, and then across Lake Victoria into Uganda, during the secret of the night, was quite a feat. If you have time, you can read more about their mission. I believe you will find it fascinating.

When I think about rescues, it makes me think about how God rescued me. I was in a terrible state, but God had mercy on me. He put me through a series of circumstances that would change my life forever. The fact is, we are all in a terrible state. When we are born into this world, we are all in sin. Because of the sin of Adam, we are born into a sin-nature. But when we accept the life-giving salvation of Jesus, that old sin-nature is exchanged for a new-nature. Many people have heard the term 'born-again' and this is what it is referring to. I am thankful God made a rescue possible for me.

THE WORLD IS SO BRIGHT NOW

Forest Park, in St. Louis Missouri, is one of the best city parks in the entire nation. Not only is it beautiful, but it has a wonderful history. Forest Park was the location for the 1904 Louisiana Purchase Exposition, also known as the St. Louis World's Fair. And, I recently learned, that Forest Park was also the host for the 1904 Summer Olympics. It is a marvelous park and one that residents of

St. Louis take great pride in. It is now my habit to spend a couple days each month in the Park to exercise and enjoy the Art Museum. It is a wonderful thing when we can appreciate the beautiful things around us. For me, that wasn't always the case. As I wrote earlier, I was always pretty tense and stressed with my daily life, and didn't take the time to enjoy the wonderful things around me. But now, that has changed. I now look forward to getting in my car, driving to the park, and enjoying the opportunity.

I now share something that I wrote in my journal while enjoying Forest Park. I had just ran the Hill in Forest Park 5 times and then sat to write the following, "*Now I sit alongside the lake. It is about 7:01 PM on July 23rd, 2018. Looking past the fountains on the lake, the moon sits quietly above the treetops, while the gentle breeze cools me. People pass slowly by on their paddle boats ... it is a perfect night. Usually after my run, I will go into the Art Museum and sit in the Impressionist Gallery. It is a special place. I stand and gaze at the paintings hundreds of years old and think of the artists that once stood there before the canvases. They stood there pouring themselves into the work, by capturing the heart, soul, and intimacy of creativity they were experiencing at the time.*"

For people that knew me before my conversion, they might be surprised that I could express those type of sentiments in my writing. But, thanks be to God, things in the world are bright now. When God does a work in our hearts, our eyes are opened to the beauty around us. And when that happens, a deep appreciation for the creativity of God and the creativity of his people, is made alive inside of us.

DELIGHT IN THE QUIET PLACE

I love to travel and see places. There is something very interesting to me about walking through an airport and seeing all the people coming and going. To think that at this moment, there are airports all over the world filled with people getting on planes for every imaginable destination, is amazing. And there is something spectacular about looking out of a plane window after rising above the clouds. Some may call me a wanderlust, but I just enjoy seeing places, meeting people from other countries, and learning about the cultures they live in. I am privileged to have been to many places around the world. But travel takes money and it takes time. So if you are like me, and have limited amounts of both, you have to limit where you can go and what you can see. But there is a special place we can all go that costs us nothing … well kind of. Actually, it costs us everything to really get there. What I am talking about is the place of intimacy with God. You may say, "That is not a real place!" If you have been there, you know what I am referring to. If you have not been in the precious presence of God, then believe me, you should. When I say it costs everything, what am I talking about? Well, when we consider all the things we can spend our time on, we must also consider what is important to us. Intimacy with Jesus in the quiet place of prayer is the most significant place we can visit. And I should be more accurate by saying, we shouldn't just want to visit, but we should want to abide there. We, as Christians, should desire to be in this place more than any other. When my walk with God is healthy, it is because I have been in the quiet place with Him. But when I fail to abide there, my life suffers. There are so many people looking for peace and some sense of worth in life.

If they would just spend time with God, they would find their worth and purpose. Being in the quiet place with God is not just some religious talk. It is a place where God wants to meet with you and I. In the mornings, I open my Bible and read several passages. After doing this, I spend some time in prayer and ask the Lord to carry me through the day. When I experience the presence of God during this time, it is a joy like no other. I still want to travel and see places, but as my walk with God grows, the place I want to be above all other, is with Him in prayer.

THE SHAMEFUL THRONE OF SELF

When we talk about a person being selfish, what are we really talking about? It is this selfishness that causes us so many problems. Selfishness is exhibited when we look and care at ourselves, without having regard for others. Elyse Fitzpatrick writes, *"Jesus relentlessly contrasted their outward show of religion with the "weightier matters of the law: justice and mercy and faithfulness." He wasn't terribly concerned about protecting their self-esteem when he called them hypocrites," "blind guides," and children of their "father, the devil." Why would he speak to them in such a way? For this one reason: he wanted to tear apart their self-reliance and self-confidence."* As we each grow more selfless, our attention is drawn to the greater throne of God, where true change in life can take place.

IMPOSSIBLE CHANGE BECOMES REALITY

I was thrilled to have had a conversation recently with a very good friend of mine. She had been struggling with unforgiveness and it was really causing problems with her emotional state. She was constantly getting angry and upset over things other people were doing. But after speaking to her about it, she told me she was ready to forgive the individuals that were causing her so much trouble. I knew she had been struggling with that for a long time, so when she said she was ready to change, I was very excited. Not only was she ready to make some changes in her life, but I knew that God was really working in her heart. After she told me she had come to that realization, I said to her, "That is the most amazing thing I have ever heard!" To hear of the progress that she had made in her thinking, and her willingness to forgive, brought a huge smile to my face. When we look at what God's Word says, we understand that His ways are right and His ways are good. When we live with issues for so long, it can sometimes seem like things will never change. But what seems impossible, can be possible when we get our focus on Jesus. Psalm 1:2 says, *"But his delight is in the law of the Lord, and in His law he meditates day and night."* We are not to meditate in some eastern religion fashion whereby we try to empty our minds. But rather, we are to meditate on the Word of God, filling our minds with the pure and true things of the Most High God. My life went from a state of misery to a state of expectation. And what was a debacle, has now turned into delight. You and I no longer have to endure the fear and pain of bondage to our sin, but we can be set free in the Lord. God wanted to heal me. And if you are suffering now, he wants to heal you too.

HUDSON TAYLOR'S AWAKENING

Hudson Taylor was a great missionary to China. He struggled for years with his ministry and experienced a lot of disappointment.

He doubted the mission would ever be productive and fruitful. But at a certain point in his life, he had a supernatural awakening to the fact that God was going to do a mighty work in Him. He realized he didn't have to have the strength to do it, But rather, God would do a mighty work through him! He had a tremendous transformation. Had he been a dedicated Christian prior to this time? Certainly, but now he experienced a level of power and strength like never before. Howard Taylor writes, *"Unless the missionaries being sent are transformed, they cannot deliver a transforming message. Even Hudson Taylor experienced this fact. He had known for years that he was to be more dependent on the Lord working through Him, but still was trying to work his own faith. In a biography on him written by Dr. and Mrs. Howard Taylor, they wrote the following, "No, 'the servant of the Lord must not strive', but must be willing to be led by just such indications of the Divine will, relying not on the help of man to accomplish a work of his own choosing, but on the unfailing guidance, resources, and purposes of God."*

YES, I TAKE RESPONSIBILITY

I desire to see revival in the hearts of God's people by turning wholeheartedly to Christ and forsaking the idols of Egypt. In the Old Testament, after God had delivered the Israelites out of the bondage of Egypt, the people still complained. And some of them, due to a lack of trusting God, wanted to return to Egypt. They had put more confidence in man's ways than God's. I suppose we have all been guilty of this. I know I have. But in my life, I wanted real change. I wanted to trust God and do things His way. I knew I needed heart revival. And this revival had to start within myself.

What does it really take to have a real and lasting change within ourselves? It can be very difficult. It is a sad commentary, but how many people go on a diet for several weeks or months, but to only start eating junk food again. I have been guilty of this myself. Yes, it is hard. But we have to stay focused on our goal. While most people are trying to lose weight, I was trying to gain weight. I am fortunate enough to have a metabolism that works overtime, but almost too good. So I had a goal to gain 7 pounds. And even though I wanted to gain some weight, I wanted it to be healthy weight. We can want change, but our changes need to be healthy. If we are making consistent and healthy choices over time, we will see the results we want. We have to take responsibility for our actions. How many times do you hear people complaining about others not taking responsibility? But, when I look in the mirror, I have to ask myself am I taking responsibility for mine. Am I really putting my trust in the Lord? Am I really making good and healthy choices for my body each day? Am I putting the time into my prayer life that I should? We need to examine ourselves in light of these questions.

FALSE EVIDENCE APPEARING REAL

I cannot remember where I heard this, but think it was in a Bible class somewhere. But someone used the acronym FEAR. They went on to say that it stood for False Evidence Appearing Real. I Timothy 1:7 says, *"For God hath not given us the spirit of fear, but of power, and of love, and of a sound mind."* Was it fear that caused the prophets of Jeremiah's day to fall down on their responsibilities? Did they not know the Lord themselves, and therefore were unable to distinguish Godly living from worldly living? Jeremiah wrote in Lamentations chapter 2, *"Thy prophets have seen vain and foolish things for thee; and they have not discovered thine iniquity, to turn away thy captivity; but have seen for thee false burdens and causes of banishment."*

It was a terrible cycle to have been in. The cycle of fear to control to anger was devastating. But now I didn't have to fear that any longer.

CAN I TELL YOU MY STORY?

I like to tell my story. I have said that I am ashamed of things in my past, but I am not embarrassed to talk about them. It is an amazing thing when we can share something of our past and encourage another person with it. There have been several situations where people at work will come into my office and open up about serious and intimate things in their lives. When this happens, it excites me to share my story with them. When we open up and are truthful about the things in our lives, people see that we are real. And when we are real, God can and will work through us. I am not sure whose hands this book will end up in, but I pray that God would use some of these words to point people to Jesus. And by doing so, help them through their struggles and problems. I would love nothing more than to be sharing this message of hope to many people throughout our country and around the world. Maybe God will give me an opportunity to do that. But even if this message can help a few, it will be worth it. So, I sit here and write with no fancy notions, but rather, as an offering of thanks back to God. Lord, use this as you see fit, according to your Kingdom purpose.

CHAPTER 15:

A CLEAN HEART

What liberty did confession bring to light
Through it all relationships were made right
Psalm 51 has been my daily devotion
Bringing about changes set into motion

INTENTIONAL DEVOTION

During the time of getting my life settled, I spent a lot of time in
Psalm 51: *Have mercy on me, O God, According to Your loving kind-*
ness, According to the multitude of Your tender mercies, Blot out my
transgressions. Wash me thoroughly from my iniquity, And cleanse me
from my sin. For I acknowledge my transgressions, And my sin is always
before me. Against You, You only, have I sinned. And done this evil in
Your sight - That You may be found just when You speak, And blameless
when You judge. Behold, I was brought forth in iniquity, And in sin
my mother conceived me. Behold, You desire truth in the inward parts,

And in the hidden part You will make me to know wisdom. Purge me with hyssop, and I shall be clean; Wash me, and I shall be whiter than snow, Make me hear joy and gladness, That the bones You have broken may rejoice. Hide Your face from my sins, And blot out all my iniquities. Create in me a clean heart, O God, And renew a steadfast spirit within me. Do not cast me away from Your presence, And do not take Your Holy Spirit from me. Restore to me the joy of Your salvation, And uphold me by Your generous Spirit. Then I will teach transgressors Your ways, And sinners shall be converted to You. Deliver me from the guilt of bloodshed O God, The God of my salvation, And my tongue shall sing aloud of Your righteousness. O Lord, open my lips, And my mouth shall show forth Your praise. For You do not desire sacrifice, or else I would give it; You do not delight in burnt offering. The sacrifices of God are a broken spirit, A broken and a contrite heart – These, O God, You will not despise. Do good in Your good pleasure to Zion; Build the walls of Jerusalem. Then You shall be pleased with the sacrifices of righteousness, With burnt offering and whole burnt offering; Then they shall offer bulls on Your altar." It helped me keep my focus in the right place. I am thankful for God's Word to comfort each day.

WE HAVE BEEN ADOPTED

During one of my trips to India, I stood on the observatory level of a luxurious high-rise hotel and took a breath of the smog-filled air and looked out over the poverty- stricken areas of the mega-city. The stark contrast hit me deeply, while behind me and through the heavy glass doors were business executives and wealthy world travelers conducting business and enjoying themselves. Inside, the world seemed new and clean, but outside, the reality was very

different. During this brief moment, thoughts that had been cul-
minating over the past years came to a fresh realization. In His
infinite wisdom, God was showing me what adoption really meant.
Not only what it meant to me personally, but how it could be proclaimed to others that needed to know the love and saving work of
the Lord Jesus. The time I spent in the adoption ministry had quite
an impact on me. Not only was I involved with many children in
need of good families and homes, but I saw more clearly the Biblical
meaning of adoption in spiritual and practical terms. We see the
pattern for adopting an earthly child pictured in God's adoption
of us through His Son Jesus. As we desire children to be adopted
in a solid and loving family, so also does God want us adopted into
His family. What an inheritance we have as joint-heirs with Christ
Himself! Romans 8:16-17 reads, *"The Spirit itself beareth witness
with our spirit, that we are the children of God: And if children, then
heirs; heirs of God, and joint-heirs with Christ; if so be that we suffer
with him, that we maybe also glorified together."*

CONFESS, AND BE SET FREE

Seeing changes in people's lives is so rewarding. Prior to her adoption, my daughter Leah experienced many challenges and struggles in her life. She was classified as a lost and found child by the
orphanage in India. I do not know all of her history, but I do know
she was on the streets in Maharashtra, India at a very young age.
At some point she was picked up by the local police and taken to
an orphanage. After being in that orphanage for about a year, she
was then transferred to Bal Asha Trust Orphanage in Mumbai,
India. So for years, Leah had been out on the streets and then in

orphanages. When she was seven years old, she was adopted into our family. We all have a lot of baggage, but for Leah, her troubles were many and deeply rooted. It was quite a stressful time in our home. The trouble we experienced was almost indescribable. I will not go into all the details, but I must say it was very difficult. Over the past couple of months, I asked Leah if I could share a couple stories about her. And please know that she is now a wonderful young lady. But like so many of us, she had her issues and it is by the grace of God she is where she is today.

On one occasion, I was laying in my bed almost asleep and heard the sound of an aluminum soda can dropping onto another soda can in the case. It is a distinct sound, so there was no mistaking the fact that someone was up in the night getting a soda. I immediately jumped out of bed, ran through the sitting room, then the kitchen, and then down the hallway to Leah's room. She was laying in bed pretending to be asleep. It was amazing how good she was at sneaking around and moving so quietly and quickly when she needed to. By the time I arrived to her room, she had already gotten into her bed, pulled the covers on herself, and was laying there peacefully. I asked her, "Leah, where is the soda?" And then in the usually way, she responded, "What soda?" With that said, I started looking around the room and after a few minutes, discovered the soda can under some clothes in the corner laundry basket. So not only had she made it back to bed, but she had also concealed the can. I held up the can, and then the admission was undeniable. But it was just one more experience in a continual stream of crazy incidents. Then like usual, we just went back to bed.

Despite all the craziness that took place over those years, today, Leah is a faithful follower of the Lord Jesus. There were so many times when I thought it was simply hopeless. But we continued on in faith, knowing that God had brought her into our family's life and that He had a plan for her. I love Leah. She is always calling me to see how I am doing and prays for me all the time. What a blessing it is when God works in our life to correct us and mold us into the people He wants us to be. Relationships are made right when God is in the middle. And I am so thankful He has worked in us. It is by His grace we have been made whole and it is by His grace we are saved. Watchman Nee wrote, *"A clear conscience is never based upon our attainment; it can only be based on the work of the Lord Jesus in the shedding of His blood."* I am thankful our minds are now clear of all those troubles from the past.

THE SPONGE RUNNING CLEAR

As I stand at the sink and wash the dishes, it is obvious the clean water has a very specific effect on the sponge. After scrubbing the mess off of the plates and dishes, the sponge takes on quite a nasty character. Let the example serve as a sort of sin in our life. It is not a pretty site, and while most of the residue has washed down the drain, the sponge remains filthy, grimy, and really quite gross. I would assume at this point in the process, most people do not put the sponge back on the sink in it's unclean state. I am guessing most people will run clean water over the sponge to clean it. Clean water is really an amazing thing. If we simply hold the sponge under the clean water, we will notice the dirt and impurities start to run out. It is a simply illustration, but I suspect one that most can relate to. We are the sponge, the grime is sin, and the water is the Life of

Christ. If we would take as much time to put ourselves under the cleansing water of Jesus, as we do the sponge every evening, what a difference it would make. When we allow the cleaning life water of Jesus to run over us, He will start flushing out all of that old junk … preparing us to be used again.

CHOOSING GOD REGARDLESS OF THE CONSEQUENCES

One of my pastor friends, Gaylon Vinson, invited me on a teaching trip to Kenya in early 2014. It was during our travel to Nairobi that we had a long layover in Amsterdam. If I recall, the layover was almost eleven hours, which was plenty of time to leave the airport and see something. If you are familiar with the movie, *The Hiding Place*, then you are familiar with the ten Boom family. Corrie ten Boom and her family lived in a suburb of Amsterdam called Haarlem. It was during the invasion of Holland by the Nazis in World War II that the family found themselves at a point of decision. The Nazis were rounding up the Jews all around Holland and many Jewish people sought refuge wherever they could find it. The ten Boom family worked with an underground network of people to house and transport people to safety out of the country. Their home was a stopover place for people in transit trying to escape the horrific Holocaust that took so many millions of precious lives.

Gaylon found something to eat and took a comfortable seat in the KLM/Northwest lounge to rest, and I went exploring. I bought a ticket in the rail station under the airport, and over the course of the next 45 minutes, and two trains later, I was within walking distance of the house that Corrie and her family had lived in. The upper levels of the home are now a museum. The lower level is now a watch store, in similar fashion as it was when the family ran their watchmakers shop out of it. The building now stands as a testimony and honor to the family that chose God's way regardless of the consequences. Sadly, the family was eventually rounded up by the Germans and sent to concentration camps themselves. Corrie's father and sister died in the camps, but Corrie survived. By some "clerical error" she was released from the camp. Prior to her death on her birthday, April 15, 1983, she enjoyed ministering to people around the world. She would tell people it was truly an act of God. After her release, she wrote many books and traveled to many places sharing her family's story and telling others about the Grace of the Lord Jesus.

On the upper level of the home is where Corrie's bedroom was. The underground network helped them build another wall behind her bed, creating a secret hiding place. There was a hidden door that allowed people to enter the Hiding Place. They ran drills and when the enemy was approaching, the refuge seeking Jews would hide in that space behind her bedroom wall. I do not remember how many people that helped save. But generations of people now know their story and many Jewish people are alive because of it. While there, I entered the space behind her bed, and stood there for a few moments in silence. What happened there was real. What happened there was special. What happened there cannot be denied … they helped when the consequences were grave. They were Psalm 51 people, that had known the Lord, and were then helping to share that love. What a testimony!

THEY PAID THE PRICE

The pastor Norman Grubb wrote the following, *"When I think about missions, I think about C. T. Studd. Alfred B. Buxton, Studd's co-pioneer in the heart of Africa, made the following comment, "C. T.'s life stands as some rugged Gibraltar – a sign to all succeeding generations that it is worthwhile to lose all this world can offer and stake everything on the world to come. His life will be an eternal rebuke to easy-going Christianity. He has demonstrated what it means to follow Christ without counting the cost and without looking back."*

People often ask "why do adoptions cost so much?" This is a good question and one I have wrestled with and have directly experienced multiple times on a personal level. When people would ask me this question, I would always give them a brief explanation of adoption agency overhead requirements, government costs, foreign agency costs, travel, etc. But I would also take that question as an opportunity to explain something else. I would share the Gospel with them, sharing how Jesus paid the ultimate price to provide a way that we might be adopted. How much did it cost Christ? It cost Him everything!

But even when we as believers adopt children, they may or may not accept all that we are trying to give them. The child may not believe our intentions. Maybe they do not accept our love. Maybe they will still not trust us. In the same sense, I suspect that God might also ask, "Why doesn't this once-orphaned child accept all that I intend for them? Many people will make a decision to go with their new Father in the sense that thy have made a profession of faith, but then stop short of accepting their new identity in Him. The transformation process of a person going from an un-regenerated person to a regenerated person is an exchange. It is a working of the power of God. Galatians 2:20 says, *"I am crucified with Christ; nevertheless, I live; yet not I, but Christ liveth in me; and the life which I now live in the flesh I live by faith in the Son of God, who loved me, and gave himself for me."* Once we have accepted the Life of Christ for our own, we are a new creation in Christ. When this happens, our ideas and motives change, and we take on thoughts of God's ways and His desires.

LIVING LIFE

The struggle is real and I suspect we all face it. Or at least some of us do. Maybe we have trouble with certain relationships, and no matter how much we want to change, it seems impossible. When I started to confess my issues, my ability to relate to others became easier. And through the confession of my issues, the desire to change and improve my relationships started to grow. When I think about relationships improving, a wonderful person comes to mind that has a special place in my heart. Yanching and her daughter had been having trouble for years. Because of trouble in their home and stress in her marriage, hurtful things would be said, and anger would often be exchanged. And just as was the case in my situation, they would find themselves in arguments. It was a vicious cycle that always left them feeling hurt and disappointed. As our relationship grew, I started telling her about my own struggles and the problems I experienced in my former marriage. It was during these many sincere conversations that she and I developed a connection. I told her I was impressed that she wanted to change. She told me about the fight going on inside of her. It was an internal struggle in her heart, and I could relate to that having gone through the same things. We would talk about family dynamics and how to better communicate with our children. When certain situations would arise, she would ask my advice on how to respond to her daughter. Over time, she started noticing a difference in their relationship. What a joyous time it has been now that there is more peace between them than ever before. Not only is their relationship improving, but she feels so much freedom and comfort in her heart. Of course, the relationship is still being healed and mended, but we are thankful for the new start for both of them. It is a blessing from God when our relationships grow in the way God intended them to be … peaceful, caring, giving, understanding, and loving. As I write this, I thank God for the healing process He is taking them through. And I pray it will continue each and every day.

I have learned a lot of things through my struggles and now it is a joy to be able to share and help others. In the early chapters of this book, I mentioned the desire to help people. I am thankful that my story and experiences, good and bad, can help. Regardless of what we are going through, God will use it in mighty ways if we will surrender to His purpose.

GOTTA TELL SOMEBODY

John Stott writes, "*The crucial question we should ask, therefore, is a different one. It is not why God finds it difficult to forgive, but how he finds it possible to do so at all. As Emil Brunner put it, "Forgiveness is the very opposite of anything which can be taken for granted. Nothing is less obvious than forgiveness." Or, in the words of Carnegie Simpson, "forgiveness is to man the plainest of duties, to God it is the profoundest of problems." The problem of forgiveness is constituted by the inevitable collision between divine perfection and human rebellion, between God as He is and us as we are."* So when I think about the forgiveness Jesus has made possible for me, I am thankful. Will you be thankful today for the forgiveness that is available because of and through Jesus Christ? I hope you will.

CHAPTER 16:

ABIDING STILL

From fleshly effort and working I cease
With a loving yoke, God guides with ease
Abiding in His presence is now my desire
Righteous by faith from this purifying fire

STAY THE COURSE

When things get difficult, it is so easy to want to quit. Several years ago, I ran a few marathons. I can't say I really ran them, because I had to do a little walking. But I least I can say I survived the distance. I have a lot of respect for people that can run a marathon well. The discipline and commitment that goes into training for that distance is remarkable. I had always wanted to run a marathon. Not because I really enjoyed running that much, but because I wanted to feel some sense of accomplishment. And don't get me wrong, completing the distance is an accomplishment. But for me,

I was trying to find some satisfaction in my performance. It was honestly a misguided effort, thinking that by completing a marathon, I would somehow feel more complete. When we do things to try and fill a void in our life, it only adds to the frustration. I know that, because after I had run 3 marathons in twelve months, I still felt the same. At that time in my life, I was still searching for security and purpose. Unfortunately, running 26.2 miles on a Sunday morning in Chicago did not really help. God wants us to rest in Him. I was trying to rest in my abilities. I might try training for another marathon in the future, but if I do, it will be for the enjoyment of it, not trying to prove anything. In my past life, I didn't realize how restful a life in Jesus could be. I am not saying we should quit everything we are doing, but we need to examine why we are doing it.

Do we get up each morning with a clear purpose? Do we go through each day with the intent of serving God in what we are doing? When Jesus is working through us, it will feel natural. And, when we rely on Christ to do the work in and through us, we will have a greater commitment to stay on task. Adoniram Judson was one of the first people to leave America to be a missionary in a foreign land. He went to Burma, now known as Myanmar, in a day in which it was very difficult. He was called by God, and even though he was committed, he fought the temptation to return home. In his book on Judson, William McElrath wrote, *"He once confessed that he had an almost uncontrollable longing to board every homeward-bound ship in the harbor...but Christ's calling had kept him on the job in Burma."*

PRAYERS ARE IN ORDER

My uncle Jack was a music minister for years. Prior to one of my trips, he wrote me a nice letter and told me that "prayers were in order." On a trip to Russia to adopt my son, I had a long flight from Moscow to Vladivostok, where he was in the orphanage. There was a couple from San Antonio that met up with us in Moscow. When we departed Moscow, we figured it would be about an 8-hour flight to the East Coast of Russia. We boarded the plane and it was more like being on an old bus. There were no doors on the overhead bins, so everything was basically sitting on the shelves above our heads. And there wasn't any safety briefing before take-off. The flight attendant seemed to have taken a quick head count and then we were off. We soon realized we were the only English-speaking people on the plane. Not even the flight attendants could communicate with us. So that seemed a little strange.

Little did we know, but our coordinator back in Moscow had bought us super-cheap tickets. Apparently, he then pocketed the rest of our money for himself. At some point, the man traveling from San Antonio got up to go use the restroom. When he returned, he laughed to me about the lavatory and said, "Wow, I have seen cleaner port-a-potties at a rock concert!" And the trip would then get even more interesting. We were uninformed that there was a layover in Krasnoyarsk, Siberia. When we started to feel the plane slowing and going into a descent, I looked at my watch and realized we had only been traveling for about 4 hours. So I knew we were only halfway there. And no one could tell us what was happening. When we landed, the flight attendants instructed us to get off. It was all very confusing. We walked down the steps from the plane into the frigid Siberian below-zero temperature. Everyone loaded into an old cattle trailer that was being pulled by a tractor. We really had no choice but to follow the crowd.

After riding in that freezing cold trailer for what seemed a long time, we came to a stop near a parking lot. Everyone got off the trailer and walked across the parking lot, getting into their cars. The four of us were left standing there alone. It was at that moment I remembered Uncle Jack's letter and another note of encouragement from a friend named Gary. Yes, prayers were in order and at that moment, my anxiety washed away. I was so encouraged by this and will always be thankful for their words. It's interesting what comes to mind when we are in a difficult situation. In that case, I knew that people were praying for us back home, and we would be alright.

We eventually found our way to another terminal at the other side of the parking lot. After stumbling around in the terminal for a while, we found the gate for our next flight. Fortunately, we had about an hour to spare. The rest of the trip was certainly an adventure, but we were at peace. I sure am thankful that God knows what He is doing! I have times of anxiety in my life, but thankfully, I always come back to the knowledge that God is looking over me. For people without a faith and hope in God, I cannot imagine how they get through the struggles of life. I can only pray that one day they will. He guides us with a loving yoke, and I am thankful for that.

ONLY ONE TRUE REALITY

In one of his sermons, Pastor Richard Rhea said, *"It's the flesh that got us into this problem; it's not going to be the flesh that gets us out of this problem."* I am thankful for his consistent messages on the Life of Jesus in our lives. Everything really comes down to one thing. Actually, it is One Person, and that is Jesus Christ. As I think about what I have written so far in this manuscript, it seems to me that I might be saying the same thing over and over again. Maybe that is true. Maybe the idea is to convey the wonderful saving Grace of Jesus in as many examples as possible. I pray the reader would find a connection with one of them and have their hearts opened to who Jesus is. What Rhea said is so true. Our problem is our flesh, so our flesh will not be the solution. The solution to our problems and every other problem, is Jesus Himself. It is so easy to get distracted by other worldly ideas, but if we keep our sights fixed on Him, we will not get aimlessly tossed here and there. We as believers should not simply be presenting another idea in the competing world of ideas. But instead, we should be sharing and exemplifying The Idea.

LORD, HELP THEM SEE

David Brainerd, a missionary to the Indians, wrote, *"I never saw the work of God appear so independent of means as at this time. I discoursed to the Native Americans, and spoke what, I suppose, had a proper tendency to promote convictions. But God's manner of working upon them appeared so entirely supernatural and above human means that I could scarce believe He used me as an instrument, or what I spake as means of carrying His work...I seem to do nothing, and indeed to have nothing to do, but to "stand still and see the salvation of God."*

I found myself obliged and delighted to say, "Not unto us," not unto instruments and means, "but to thy name be glory." What a wonderful testimony by Brainerd, realizing his work was to be present, to share the Word, and to watch God move upon the hearts of those whom he was with. Let us be careful not to put the responsibility upon ourselves to save a human soul, but instead, look to the Lord Himself to do the work. I Corinthians 3:7 says, *"So then neither he who plants is anything, nor he who waters, but God who gives the increase."* So here we find in Scripture a wonderful foundational truth. We are to plant and water, but it is God who brings about life. What a relief this truth can be to the person that has been struggling to take on the sins and problems of others. The yoke of the Lord is easy and He will work through our individual giftings as we yield ourselves to Him.

WHAT IS THE WORK?

Several years ago, I had the opportunity to travel to Morocco. It was a fascinating trip that took me through Dubai and into Casablanca. I then took a train to Fez. The old city of Fez was an amazing place with many narrow streets and busy markets. There was so much activity everywhere and the people were friendly. While drinking some mint tea at a small sidewalk café in Fez, I watched as some men opened their shops and then captured a photo of a woman holding her children's hands while walking through the market. The thought occurred to me that most people are simply trying to get through their life in peace. They want to work and provide for their families, and enjoy themselves while doing it.

Following that visit to an Islamic nation, my prayer time was focused on the serious and comprehensive role their faith played in their lives versus the often compartmentalized and somewhat mediocre commitment we sometimes see in our Christian faith. It is a serious thing we have been called into. We are called to run this race of faith to win. It is this race of life that we so often run distracted by false hopes and motivations. It is my desire to be encouraging and thought provoking, and by no means condemning. So I hope I can run this race to win with the love of Christ, encouraging others to keep going. I may not agree with other religions, but I can love the people. I can share the love and hope of Jesus, and then see what results He brings. When we understand that it is God Himself who really makes things happen, it takes the stress and worry off of us. I am thankful to have come to that realization in my life.

I used to find myself trying to figure out what God wanted from me. It was an on-going question that plagued me for years. I kept thinking there must be more to my Christian walk than this. I thought I needed to achieve something or be something special. But then I came to the realization and awareness of what the Scripture was actually teaching. John 6:28-29 says, *"Then they said to Him, 'What shall we do, that we may work the works of God?' Jesus answered and said to them, 'This is the work of God, that you believe in Him whom He sent.'"*

Jesus told the disciples to simply, "Believe in me." That was their work. Regardless of what we are going through in life, our main work is to believe in the Lord Jesus. And that believing is not simply a casual head-knowledge. Believing in Jesus goes beyond a simple awareness and should include trusting and having faith in

Him. When we do this, He makes things clear in our lives. When we are truly believing in Jesus, our conscience can be clear. We get ourselves into a lot of problems when trying to work in our flesh. But when we look to Him, the Spirit will work through our problems, and we will finally begin running in a way that pleases Him.

TOSSED TO AND FRO

It seems the battle would never stop. Have you ever had a relentless headache that seemed to have no cure? I have never had much trouble with headaches, but know people who have. It is a terrible thing to be in pain and agony with no relief. But I had another kind of ache. There were many times I felt like I was going crazy. In my past, my emotions were so out of control. I would be up one day and then down the next. And sometimes it wasn't just day by day, but worse, hour by hour. If I would have gone to doctor, who knows what they would have diagnosed me with. Ultimately, I was not putting my faith in the Lord. I was running here and there in my mind trying to get some peace. I just could not get my mental focus that I knew I needed. Ephesians 4:14-15 says, *"that we should no longer be children, tossed to and fro and carried about with every wind of doctrine, by the trickery of men, in the cunning craftiness of deceitful plotting, but, speaking the truth in love, may grow up in all things into Him who is the head – Christ."* God wants us to, in a spiritual sense, grow up. He does not want us to remain as children that have no understanding. But instead, He wants us to lean into His Word and stand up in faith. We can be secure in God. Nothing else will bring us to a place of security but Him. T. Austin Sparks wrote, *"The mark of a life governed by the Holy Spirit is that such a life is continually and ever more occupied with Christ."*

Charles Trumbull writes, "*Jesus Christ does not want to be our helper; He wants to be our life. He does not want us to work for Him. He wants us to let Him do His work through us, using us as we use a pencil to write with - better still, using us as one of the fingers on His hand. When our life is not only Christ's but Christ, our life will be a winning life; for He cannot fail. And a winning life is a fruit-bearing life, a serving life.*"

A LOVING HEAVENLY FATHER

I can remember going into the children's rooms every night before bedtime and saying a prayer with them. It was always a great way to end the day. They would sometimes ask me to read them a book or tell them a story. They seemed to like hearing me tell them stories. I hope my children look back on their childhood and have some good memories of these times. Even though I made my fair share of parenting mistakes, I believe they would be able to say that I wanted to be a loving father. When I did make a mistake with them, I would apologize. But as much as I wanted to be a loving father, I still had my limitations. Not everyone has had good childhood memories. And some people have had awful experiences in their childhood. I am so thankful we have a loving Father in heaven that loves us no matter what has happened. His love is without fail and it never ends. When we realize how much God loves us, we will rest in Him just like my children did with me during those precious goodnight prayers.

CHAPTER 17:

THE HEALER

Now complete and secure in Christ alone
No more fear and anxiety in my home
Many years to get past hurt feelings
This servant now knows true healing

NO MORE FEAR

I am an introvert by nature, but I do enjoy interacting with people, especially when I think I can be of some help. On a flight from Amman, Jordan, to Chicago, I sat next to an older woman carrying a Saudi passport. As we took our seats and prepared to takeoff, I looked over and noticed her nervously fidgeting with her purse and some paperwork. As we taxied to the runway and then started our takeoff, she was tightly clutching the seat armrest. She was obviously scared of flying. I tried saying a few things to her, but she did not speak English. After we were in the air, we went through a couple patches of rough turbulence and she was visibly frightened. At that point, I reached over to her and gently put my hand on her forearm, and then smiled at her while given an assuring nod of confidence. My heart felt for her and I wanted to kindly let her know we would be alright. The turbulence didn't last long, and after a few minutes the flight was smoother. Several minutes later, after she felt settled again, she reached into her purse and dug around a bit, and then pulled out a small candy bar. She then looked over at me smiling, and gave me the candy bar with a gracious nod of her own. We couldn't speak each other's language, but we interacted by caring and sharing with each other. We didn't know each other's names, and would never see each other again. But I will always remember that moment. The wrapper of that candy bar is now in the pages of my Bible. Every time I flip through those pages and see it, I say a prayer for her and have to smile. That moment on the plane my not seem significant to some, but for me it was an important moment. It was just a small example of how helping someone can bring joy. Even if only a smile or a reassuring nod, we can help people out of their fear or whatever may be holding them in bondage.

RELINQUISH MY RIGHTS

Before I traveled to Kenya to live and work as a missionary, the mission board required me to attend a missionary training center. The goal of the training was to prepare to live overseas while not getting overwhelmed by the culture shock. There are so many different things to consider when moving overseas and some people struggle with the transition. Living in a foreign country can be challenging if one is not prepared. Some people adapt well, while others really struggle. There are a lot of things to consider. For starters, you are away from family and familiar surroundings. And not only do you have to learn your way around the new country, but you also have to contend with language barriers, cultural differences, driving, eating, etc. And depending on how harsh the living conditions are, one can quickly become very stressed. At one of the training sessions I attended, the instructor gave each person a paper titled, *I Relinquish My Rights*. In order to adjust to the other culture and have a smooth transition, we had to relinquish our rights to a variety of things. Ultimately, if we are going to succeed in a foreign land to where we are traveling, we have to give up our rights to have things the way we want them.

Oswald Chambers wrote, *"There will have to be the relinquishing of my claim to my right to myself in every phase. Am I willing to relinquish my hold on all I possess, my hold on my affections, and on everything, and to be identified with the death of Jesus Christ? There is always a sharp painful disillusionment to go through before we relinquish. When a man really sees himself as the Lord sees him, it is not the abominable sins of the flesh that shock him, but the awful nature of the pride of his own heart against Jesus Christ."*

MENTAL COMBAT

There is a battle for the minds and hearts of people today. When one walks into a bookstore, they can walk up and down each aisle and peruse all the different titles. And one will find that between each cover is a set of ideas and thoughts the author came to realize and then share. Whether the author was in complete agreement with what he or she wrote, thoughts they were once unaware of had become knowledge to them. When we pick up a book, we are not just reading type on the page, but we are partaking of what that author is trying to convey. Sometimes those thoughts are healthy and sometimes those thoughts are not. Some books are pleasing to God and some are not. I suppose it depends on a person's outlook and what they deem as important. There are so many messages out there today, how can one know what is real? I certainly believe the Bible is real and it is God's message for us. Not only can we read the Bible to find out what God desires and expects of us, but we can read the Bible in a way to protect us as well. If one believes the Bible is true, and spends enough time reading it, then that person will recognize the misguided teachings in other things that are read. If we do not have a firm foundation in God's Word, then we can easily be misguided by other things we read. Ideally, we should read everything through the filter of Scripture. And not only should we be careful what we consume, but we should be equally, or more concerned, about what we let our children read and consume. Tedd Tripp writes, *"I am interested in helping parents engage in hand-to-hand combat on the world's smallest battlefield, the child's heart."* When we realize there is a battle for our hearts and minds, we can look to God and take refuge in Him. The result will be freedom from fear and anxiety. Praise God for that! It really is important to have our minds saturated with the Word of God so we can easily recognize fallacies in the almost unlimited marketplace of ideas.

HARD LESSONS FOR THE IRON MAN

Life is not always easy, but if we pay attention, we can learn a lot of good lessons. A friend and I would occasionally visit an acquaintance of ours over coffee and donuts. This gentleman lived in the country with his wife on a 40-acre piece of property he was very proud of. It was a little drive to get there, but after the trip, we always felt comfortable in their home. He and his wife would always have the coffee on and were excited to see us. In the winter, Bob would always have a nice fire going in their living room woodstove. He told us once that when he was younger, he was often cold, so he kept a 7-year supply of firewood on hand. He had a very rough childhood and loved to tell some of his stories. At the age of 14, his father walked him to the end of their driveway and said, "Son, there is the world, now you can go have it." With that, Bob took off on his own. He would eventually partner up with his uncle, riding boxcars around the country looking for work. Being a hobo wasn't easy. Bob told one story of a time when they jumped onto the wrong train. Instead of heading south, they went north. And with that, they traveled into a winter storm clinging to the outside of the train. He said they were literally frozen to it when it pulled into the train yard. Usually, they would jump off and roll into the ditch prior to entering the yard. He laughed as he told how they jumped off those trains at nearly thirty miles an hour. Being a hobo wasn't easy. On this occasion, being frozen to it, the yard bulls beat them off with sticks. He smiled and said, "Those were rough times."

His uncle was always trying to teach him something, but often in peculiar ways. They were in the Badlands of South Dakota during one of their travels. At some point, Bob realized he was alone, and Unc, as he called him, was nowhere to be found. Bob wandered around for three days scrounging for food and water, hoping to find his way out. He saw a road and starting walking down it, when there appeared a man in the distance. It was his uncle. When they met up, Bob asked Unc where he had been. His uncle told him he had been watching him the whole time and just wanted to see if he could make it. Bob learned a lot of lessons. And he usually had to learn them through difficult circumstances. Although my childhood was very simple compared to Bob's, I had to learn a lot of lessons too. But regardless of how we learned them, we both eventually found peace in our Lord and Savior Jesus. After those rough years of his youth, Bob dedicated his life to Jesus and sought to serve Him until the day he died. I am thankful to have learned from him. There comes a point at which we should be secure in the Lord. When I realized that Jesus performed a miracle in my life, it made a huge difference in my attitude. At some point during the second year of my separation, my thoughts changed. I was laying face down in my bed one night and had a thought quickly jump into my head. Instead of being upset that my wife had left, I was now thankful for what God was doing in me. Whether she was there or not didn't matter. What mattered was what God wanted to do in my life. So with that, I realized God had performed a miracle in me. I am now secure in that thought. The trouble of the past no longer plagues me like before. What a relief Jesus has given me.

THE ESSENCE OF BEAUTY

Yanching often photographs the variety of different floral arrangements she creates. Her beautiful flower art intrigues me. She can take a handful of flowers, leaves, and small branches, and create the most beautiful art from it. It is really a testimony to the wonderful heart she has. Earlier in my life, I wasn't always an admirer of art, but now my life has changed. And through this healing, there is now something very fascinating about art. We know that in the beginning God created the heavens and the earth and all that is in it. And then God said, "Let us make man in Our image." From this original creation, God instilled into each one of us different abilities and talents. When we are being creative, we are simply exhibiting one of the wonderful qualities God has enabled us with. Yanching has a special gift, and when she is utilizing her gift, she feels a sense of accomplishment. In the same sense, when I sit here and try to convey my thoughts, I feel purpose. What an amazing life God has given us. When I look around the house, and see her floral creations, I not only admire her abilities, but it takes me closer to God. I know he has a plan and purpose for each and every person. So, when we tap into that purpose, life becomes so much brighter and enjoyable. When we experience true healing in our hearts, we are seeing the hand of God at work. We are the artwork of God. When I walk past a beautiful flower now, I see God in it. I praise him for His creation, and am thankful to be a part of it.

WHAT DO YOU HAVE AGAINST HIM?

My friend had a brother-in-law that was constantly getting upset about things in the church. He would always complain about something, whether it was the music or the preaching or the hyp-ocritical people, etc. So one day the brother-in-law came into my friend's office and said he was finished with the church for good. My friend just sat and listened to him go on and on for several minutes. My friend then calmly said, *"Ok, you have all these com-plaints, but can you find anything wrong with Jesus?!"* With that, the brother-in-law said nothing, and quickly left, closing the door. The next day, around the same time in the afternoon, the brother-in-law quickly poked his head into my friend's office and said, "No, I cannot!" What is the point in telling that? The point is this, there will always be something to find fault in, but that does not relieve us of our accountability to Jesus. Just because everyone around might be doing something wrong, or maybe it just seems wrong to us, we still have an obligation to seek Jesus. When we all stand before the Lord Jesus on judgement day, he is not going to ask what John or Sally did or thought. He is going to be concerned with us as individuals. We cannot stand behind others, trying to use them as excuses for being negligent in our relationship to our Creator. It just won't work that way. The Bible says that every knee shall bow to Jesus. Let's do it now! Romans 6:23 says, *"For the wages of sin is death, but the gift of God is eternal life in Christ Jesus our Lord."* I am thankful I no longer have fear and anxiety in my home. I cannot stand behind the real or perceived faults of others. I am accountable to Him. The sin in my past brought about death, but I now enjoy the life that God has given me.

THE SUPER HERO

Victory. This is what everyone expects of a super hero. John Biegeleisen said, "*The ages speak and men refuse to listen. The stress of strain of history tell their tragic story. Pain and passion, martyrdom and destruction proclaim God's judgment. But the voice of Christ, the voice of the reign of God, is more than a voice, it is a power of redemption anchored in the Cross, which is the agony and tragedy of life ending in victory.*" But can victory through Jesus be so exclusive? Is there another way into heaven without accepting the death and resurrection of Jesus Christ? The Bible tells us that Jesus willingly submitted Himself to be crucified as a sacrifice for the sin of man and when we accept Him as Savior, we will be saved. But what about all the other beliefs? What about all the good intentions to make a life right before God through some other means? What about the fact that I am just a good person? God's Word reveals to us that Jesus willingly came to Earth and dwelt among us to carry out this heavenly mission. Jesus, the Son of God, loves us so much that He died for you and I. I can remember a time when my son Jonah was hit in the cheekbone by a Frisbee leaving his face bruised. Although this was a relatively insignificant incident, even thinking about it is not pleasant and brought feelings of hurt. No parent enjoys it when pain enters their child's life. As an earthly father, I cringe at the thought of one of my children having to endure pain, let alone submit them to it. Although this is true, if pain and sacrifice resulting in death was necessary to save all mankind, would it be worth it? Before Jesus was arrested, tried, and killed, He prayed in a place called Gethsemane and asked, "*O my Father, if it be possible, let this cup pass from me; nevertheless, not as I will, but your will be done."*

So there was Jesus asking in prayer if there was another solution, some other way. The Lord knew, in His infinite will and wisdom, there had to be a perfect and unblemished sacrifice to pay for the sin of man. Jesus, the Lamb of God, became that sacrifice and is now therefore, our Redeemer. A verse familiar to many says, *"For God so loved the world that He gave His only begotten Son."* So I will ask you this question: If there was another way into heaven or some other way that man could be made approved unto God, do you not think that Jesus would have been relieved from the Cross? Certainly, God would have spared His Son the pain and agony of an excruciating death if there was an alternative way. Jesus is alive today and He stands knocking at the door. He desires us to accept His Eternal work of the Cross. If my son is reading this … I love you Jonah!

Jesus spoke the following words, "I am the way, the truth, and the life; no man cometh unto the Father, but by me." It has been said that one's response to what Jesus declared can be taken three different ways. One can conclude that: a) Jesus was telling the truth b) Jesus was lying, or c) He was out of His mind. What do you think? I believe Jesus is telling the Truth!

CHAPTER 18:

NEW LIFE

I know my sin well and others do too
Salvation is now my joy through and through
No longer are there sins to hide
Once dry bones have come alive inside

BREATHING CLEAN AIR

A.W. Tozer said, *"Let any man turn to God in earnest, let him begin to exercise himself unto godliness, let him seek to develop his powers of spiritual receptivity by trust and obedience and humility, and the results will exceed anything he may have hoped in his leaner and weaker days."*

I feel as though my old life was like living in a smoke-filled room. I was never a smoker, but I know a lot of people who are. It would seem the longer a person stays in a smoke-filled room, the harder it would be to remember what clean air felt like to breathe. And it is quite possible that some may not have ever breathed clean air. Using the smoke analogy, when I think about my old life, it was as if our family lived in a smoke-filled house. Did we just get used it? I don't think so. Being in a space without clean breathing air is suffocating and one trying to breathe can never operate at the capacity they were intended to. So, it goes without saying, that is not a good way to live. How much time is wasted by all of us in smoke-filled rooms when we need to get out. After the separation, the smoke cleared, and family members started to breathe clean air again. It is my opinion, that when a spouse experiences such clean breathing air in their new environment, they may just decide to never go back.

So what is so significant about what Tozier writes above? Please read his quote again slowly and examine what he is saying. My past life was filled with leaner and weaker days. But after the healing process began, the smoke began to clear, and I started breathing again. Breathing the way God intended me to. When we are obedient to God and living in humility, our spiritual receptivity will allow God to flow through us in a way that will not only transform us, but will impact those around us.

HOPE AND GRACE JUST GO TOGETHER

When I think about rejoicing and gladness, I think about my daughters Hope and Grace. Grace is a people-magnet and is always smiling. Grace was adopted from India when she was 6-years old. At the age of 2, she had spiral meningitis and it paralyzed the right side of her body. She made a partial recovery, but still limps and has some speech difficulties. She is a sweet and kind young lady that I am proud of. She loves to visit with people and always gives a big hug. Grace, because of her physical handicaps, will always need some assistance in life, but she is joyful. No matter what happens to us in life, we can be joyful. It is a good thing that joy is not simply an emotion. But rather, joy is a fruit of the Spirit. We can have hope in the Grace of God! And where there is Grace, there is Hope. Hope is another daughter of mine. Hope and Grace were adopted at the same time. I can remember Hope wrapped up in a jacket sitting in the airport working on her coloring books as we waited for our departure home. I will never forget Hope leaving the orphanage. She walked out of the orphanage and never turned to look back. I remember telling her in the cab, to make sure she waved goodbye to her caregivers. When I think about Hope, she reminds me that in Christ, we have no need to turn back. Our past is past and we can each look forward to a new tomorrow. Praise God for that! In the truest sense of the words, Hope and Grace go together! Even God's creation rejoices. Psalm 96:11-13 says, *"Let the heavens rejoice, and let the earth be glad; Let the sea roar, and all its fullness; Let the field be joyful, and all that is in it. Then all the trees of the woods will rejoice before the LORD. For He is coming, for He is coming to judge the earth. He shall judge the world with righteousness, And the peoples with His truth."*

WE ARE SAINTS

I always thought my grandparents were great people. Grandpa would often sit in the backyard under a shade tree and have a glass of lemonade in the summer. He really knew how to relax. At least that is how I remember him. And if I remember correctly, I never saw him get upset. Grandma would always offer a snack and had the ability to put a nice meal together very quickly. We played cards, watched baseball games, went fishing, and enjoyed our visits in the backyard. We would sit in their backyard after I mowed the grass and enjoy a cool drink together. Grandpa would often encourage me in the Lord and ask when I was going to be baptized. He didn't pry into my personal life too much, but he was always so encouraging. I would consider my grandparents saints. I know they had their faults, but in my eyes, they were great people. But what really makes a person a saint? My grandparents really were saints, but not because of all the nice things they did for me. No, they were saints because of their relationship with Jesus. The Bible teaches us that those having a life in Jesus are saints. Nothing more and nothing less will meet the criteria. The saint will have a burning desire to seek God in all things. Ron Marr writes, *"Ours must be a God-given intensity of spirit that demands that all else give way to the work God is doing in us. It must refuse to be derailed from seeking Him, the things of His realm of the eternal and spiritual, and His glory and praise. Ours must be a determination born within by the Spirit to know Him in glorious intimacy, a Spirit-born determination never to stop seeking Him, no matter the extent of our failure to find Him as we would like, a determination never to stop until He reveals Himself in us, us in Him, in present peace and joy in spite of the surrounding terror."*

ONLY TWO KINDS OF PEOPLE

After the 1992 Vice Presidential debate, Admiral William Stockdale got a lot of criticism for his debate performance. Many mocked him and poked fun at his comments, *"Who am I, Why am I here?"* and *"Gridlock!"* It was a somewhat unflattering time for him on that stage, but Stockdale was a highly decorated Naval veteran and Vietnam prisoner of war survivor. Sometimes people are judged based on a single moment in time when we should be looking at them more fairly. Stockdale was a brilliant man, a dedicated and loyal service member of our country, and Medal of Honor recipient. Everyone has a story, but sometimes we need to look a little deeper to figure out what it is. Someone like Stockdale had lived his entire life accomplishing good things, but then was ridiculed because of one evening. He would later comment in an interview about his opening line, "Who am I, Why am I here?" He said he never had the opportunity in the debate to get back to those answers. Some of us will never get a chance to explain ourselves, but we can rest assured that God knows everything about us and he is compassionate. When we look at a person, we have very limited information about who they are or what their history may have been. We should each view one another in love and humility. When we do this, our understanding for one another will increase, and our problems can be avoided much easier. But even if we are not treated fairly by others, we can be completely secure in Jesus. So much in life in unstable, so our security must rest on Him.

Dietrich Bonhoeffer said, *"The disciple is thrown out of the relative security of life into complete insecurity, which is trust in absolute security and protection in community with Jesus."* Each day, I have to ask myself which type of person will I be. Will I be that person that is clinging to security in earthly things, or will I be the type of person clinging to the One who is secure? Will I be like those that mocked Admiral Stockdale or will I desire to know people for who they really are?

WORSHIPPING THE UNKNOWN GOD

Ray, a former boss of mine, and I attended an electronics trade show in Taipei, Taiwan. We were looking for small motors and a battery supplier for our motion displays we manufactured for the advertising industry. The show we were attending was three days and we spent another two days looking at equipment manufacturers in the neighboring Taiwanese cities. I can remember driving through the Taiwanese countryside watching farmers in the rice fields and being excited about the whole experience. After visiting a few factories, our driver and interpreter took us to a temple they thought we might like. As I stood in that temple in the heart of Taipei, I was amazed by the dedication of the people, but I also wondered if they knew who God really was. They were all going through the rituals with prayers and incense, and in my mind, I was asking Jesus to reveal Himself to them. If I really believed that God gives the increase, then surely He must do that kind of work also. If you are a Christian and have had the opportunity to travel to other countries, where Christianity is in the minority, then maybe you can relate to what I was feeling. I do not want to condemn anyone. That is not my responsibility. But I have chosen to believe the Word of God to be true. And in the Bible, it states that there is only One Mediator between God and man, and that Person is Jesus Christ. So what good does it do to partake of religious rituals and customs, if it does not lead a person to Jesus? I believe the enemy has succeeded in confusing and deceiving many people. When I was in that temple, I felt a love for the people. But with that love comes a desire to tell them who I believe Jesus is and how He can help them. Some may fault me for doing that, but that is what God calls us to do in obedience to His Word. Since that trip, I have encountered other similar situations. I will often share my faith, and if people are interested in hearing more, I gladly share with them. If not, I walk away knowing I tried in love, to share God the best I know how.

BETTER BECAUSE OF IT

For someone reading this that has gone through a separation or a divorce, I want you to know that things will get better. Or at least I should say, things can get better. And maybe your issue is something completely different. Regardless of what are problems are in life, there is a solution. Early on, people would always tell me it would be a process. I have written about that in previous chapters, but it is worth mentioning again. Because at every stage of my process, I was growing a little bit more. My ability to adjust and cope with the changes was getting easier over time and my ability to appreciate the days ahead also improved. Enjoying my new life stemmed from the realization that I had come from a dark place to a new and bright place. That may sound a little hokey, but it is so true. The improvement came at every step, because I chose to move forward in a good direction. Certainly, there are plenty of statistics that show people decline in life after such a traumatic event, but it doesn't have to be that way. When we have God in our life, and we choose to move forward with Him, the potential for us to accomplish great things is amazing. There is a line in the movie *Unbroken*, that says, *"A moment of pain is worth a lifetime of glory.*" Certainly, none of us want to sign up for pain, but when we experience it, God's glory will be on the other side. So it is my prayer that if you have struggled in some of the same ways I have, that you would realize your worth, realize God loves you, and take steps to let Him heal you. Your life will get better if you humble yourself before God and others. When that happens, you will begin to notice small changes in your outlook and attitude. After several months and years, you will look back and be amazed how far you have come!

WHAT ARE YOU EXCITED ABOUT TODAY?

Ezekiel 37:5 says, *"Thus says the Lord God to these bones: "Surely I will cause breath to enter into you, and you shall live."* In a remarkable picture of God's restorative power, the prophecy was set forth that God's people would have life breathed into them once again. What is once dead in sin to the world, can be revived by God's powerful and holy Word. I am friends with a couple in India that have a fantastic ministry to single mothers and orphans. They take their time to raise funds, feed, clothe, and preach the good news of Jesus to countless people each week. John and his wife Pratima are great examples of what God can do with a willing person. They have ministered to and witnessed many people come to the saving knowledge of Jesus. People that were once spiritually dry and dead to sin have had life breathed into them. Their ministry in Hyderabad, India, is a testimony to God's goodness. Having left the comforts of a corporate job, they chose to serve the Lord in this remarkable way. I am proud to have them as friends and am always encouraged by their zeal for God's work. When I think about people being excited, their loving smiles come to mind. They are truly excited to be living as examples in a world that desperately needs Godly examples.

FIGURE OUT WHAT YOUR WINNING IS

Speaker and author Simon Sinek said, *"You only have one 'why' in your entire life, and the opportunity is to live in balance, or out of balance with that. If you can figure that out, you can choose to make decisions to make that 'why' come to life."* When I think about purpose, a young man named Simon, living in Eldoret, Kenya, comes to mind. I have observed him over the past several years pour his heart out into many orphan children in his village in western Kenya. He figured out what his winning was early in life. Having been an orphan himself, he determined to help others that were in need. Through his efforts, he has been able to raise funds and build an orphanage, while feeding and providing for dozens of children. He is one of the most kind and humble people I know, always offering a word of encouragement and prayer. He will often comment how I have been helpful to them, but I think he has encouraged me more. When a person figures out what their winning is, they can then begin to work within their gifting. Simon has a gift for working with young people, and it shows. He and his young family work unselfishly to minister to those in need. When I think of Simon, I see someone who is living in balance with their calling. It is because of this faithfulness to his calling that God continues to work through him. Simon is an encouragement to me. He is not a person of lofty position, but rather, a humble young man setting out to honor God. Richard Wurmbrand said, *"Don't tell me that such a wide horizon is only for the highest church leaders, and not for rank-and-file Christians. There is no such thing as a rank-and-file Christian, because every Christian is of the highest rank. Every Christian is a partaker or the divine nature. God doesn't put anyone away in a file in the archives. There are no rank-and-file Christians. Christians think in terms of the whole cosmos and its creator, as they think in terms of infinity and eternity."*

CHAPTER 19:

THE EXCHANGE

No longer in bondage to my past
True freedom in Christ that will last
Transformation of this man by God's power
Taking steadfast refuge in his strong tower

IT IS WITH THANKS THAT I SIT HERE AND WRITE THESE words. To have another opportunity at life with a new perspective is something very special to me. As I look to the future now, I realize the things that held me captive before no longer have me in bondage. The Bible tells us when Jesus sets us free, then we are free indeed. This has become real to me. So now, I consider the future plans that God has for my life, and it gives me hope. As I contemplate the almost infinite possibilities, one thing is for certain. By staying steadfast in my relationship to Jesus, I can trust the future will be good. For the believer in God, we can trust in His mercies new every morning. By taking refuge in the tower of

God's infinite mercy, we are shielded from being overrun. However, there will still be struggles. Today has been a somewhat frustrating day. My mind kept getting distracted with a variety of things. But I kept telling myself to re-engage with my work and asked the Lord to bless it. I hope the following words will be an encouragement to you.

Where spiritual meets physical

It amazes me to think about the digital world we live in. To think that from our phones we can send and receive voice, photos, and videos is quite extraordinary. As I write this today, I am sitting in Forest Park next to the lake listening to the beautiful fountains. Looking across the lake I can see a number of people walking up and down the paths enjoying the warm afternoon. To my right and up the hill sits the Art Museum with a statue of St. Louis. What I cannot see and hear though is all the communication that is around me. If my eyes and ears had the same receptivity capability as my phone, I would probably be overwhelmed by the amount of sound and imagery around me. It is as if these digital sounds and images are everywhere at the same time. When our digital receptivity devices tap into these digital packets, they simply receive what is already there. Is that audio or image everywhere at the same time? I suppose I would need someone smarter than me to weigh in. There may be so many sounds and images around me right now that the ability to see them all would be frightening. If I am correct in my assumption about this, then this could be likened to the spiritual realm. The spiritual realm is all around us, but we just cannot see or hear it. Again, I suspect if we could, the imagery would be too fantastic and overwhelming for us to handle. It would be quite frightening. When we look at the Bible and read of accounts where angels appeared, they would say, "Do not fear." There is a reason for this. The heavenlies must be so awe-inspiring and magnificent that our human receptivity would be unable to process. When we pray, our prayers must leave our being and make contact with heaven somehow. This amazes me and I wonder when we are with the Lord, will we have a clear knowledge and understanding of this. In any event, there must be a point when the spiritual meets the physical. Engineer and scientist Chuck Missler has speculated that we are really in a digital simulation. I would not want to be dogmatic about that, but his teaching and theories are quite interesting. He makes the case that while most people would view our physical world as the real and heaven being some imaginary place, that the opposite is true. Maybe we should view heaven as the reality and not our current physical location. Regardless, I know I am here now and that is what matters. What matters most is that I am trusting in and serving God by His Grace each day.

When that spiritual realm does indeed touch us, The Spirit of God can inspire, teach, and motivate us for eternal heavenly works. From the book In His Steps, author Sheldon writes, *"Almost with the first syllable he uttered there was a distinct presence of the Spirit felt by them all. As the prayer went on, this presence grew in power. They all felt it. the room was filled with it as plainly as if it had been visible. When the prayer closed there was a silence that lasted several moments. All heads were bowed. Henry Maxwell's face was wet with tears. If an audible voice from heaven had sanctioned their pledge to follow the Master's steps, not one person present could have felt more certain of the divine blessing. And so the most serious movement ever started in the First Church of Raymond was begun."*

In Sheldon's remarkable book, we read of the miraculous activity and life-changing conversions by people that were once blinded by their selfish and sinful ways. When the Spirit of God meets us in the physical, we will certainly take on new priorities and our outlook on life will be one of expectation toward God's goodness toward us and others.

A COMPLETE OVERHAUL OF DESIRES

When our life is exchanged for a life in God we will find that our wants and desires will start changing. The things that seemed important to us in our selfishness will be exchanged for things important to God. Jonathan Edwards writes, *"For those who are indeed Christians don't belong to this world, and therefore it is very unbecoming in them to have their minds taken up about these things. The example of Paul may make all people ashamed whose minds are occupied chiefly with things of the world, about gaining estates or acquiring honors."*

Moses says a remarkable thing in chapter 33 of the book of Exodus. After all the Israelites had gone through and the history that Moses had experienced in his life, he was still resolute concerning the leading of God. In Exodus 33:15 we read the following, *"And he said unto him, If thy presence go not with me, carry us not up hence."* It is my prayer that we are that determined, as Moses was, to be dependent on God's calling and leading as we consider the multitude of options and the never-ending pursuit of goals and knowledge that many are striving for. In a world where we can take a number of endless directions and ways we live our lives, let us be as Moses – steadfast in the idea that unless the Lord's presence is with us, we shall not go.

Where Revival happens

One evangelist friend of mine would often joke how an evangelist could blow in, blow up, and blow out ... leaving the local church pastor with a huge mess. There is some humor in that but also a little truth. When people run on emotions, we get a mess. But when people are getting a true Spirit-led transformation, we have order. It was several years ago that our church had an evangelist that came to speak for several days. He was a very good preacher and brought a convicting message. He also had the ability to get people a little excited. The revival was held during 3 evenings that particular week and then the meetings were finished up on a Sunday morning. Many people came to the altar for prayer each night and there were reports of students at the neighboring school getting excited about Jesus. During the Sunday morning service on the following Sunday, our pastor gave a summary of how he felt the meetings had gone the previous week. And then he asked, "How will we really know the results of what happened?" I then made the comment that we would know if people's decisions and commitments were real by the real and lasting change in behavior. We would know if we had experienced true transformation by the future actions and choices we would make. As I look at my own life, I can see that I have had some religious and emotional experiences, but they didn't always change the way I behaved or how I lived my life. Real revival happens in the heart of each of us when the convicting and nurturing Word of God takes root in us, and by doing so, results in Godly behavioral changes.

WITH GOD'S SUPPORT

Many skyscrapers are being built with large weighted devices called tuned mass dampers. They are located near the top of the building and made of concrete or steel. The dampers weigh many tons and act as a counter-balance when the different elements come. In the event of heavy winds or earthquakes, the tuned mass damper serves to provide stability in order for the structure to be protected. I have also been in buildings where the construction seemed to be weak and insufficient. At a hotel in Vladivostok, Russia, we laid there awake almost all night wondering if the windows were going to blow in. I guess one cannot expect much for thirty dollars a night, but being on the eleventh floor in a terrible storm was not the best choice. We survived the night to tell about, but I would not volunteer for that again. A structure can be built very strong or it can be built very weak. Without being too light about the subject, I have thought of Christ as being our tuned mass damper. When we have Him at our core, the various storms that come into our life will not take us down. Prayerfully, the storms that enter into our life will draw us closer to the Lord and not further from Him. We are never sure what tomorrow will bring and we must have a solid foundation and support system to endure.

A CHANGE IN PRIORITIES

Even as much as I want to surrender all to the work of Christ, I am tempted to deviate in my financial life. There is so much worry about money in life, and when we consider all that we have or don't have, it can be challenging. Keeping our finances in proper perspective is important. When I realize that everything is already God's, then it becomes easier to give Him what He deserves. And when I view myself as a conduit through which He can work, the financial part of my life makes more sense. When we consider giving money to God's work, we often think of an offering or some sort of donation. But, it would probably be better to view everything as God's. When we give our whole life to God, we give Him everything that is in it. In his book Missions in the Third Millennium, Stan Guthrie writes, *"Even when we are investing rather than spending, the consumer mindset can take over. Our treasure remains on earth, not in heaven, when we build our own balance sheets without investing in the kingdom, when we are always waiting for a better time to give, when our giving does not track our growing wealth, when we never even consider living below our means so that we can give more. Jesus, who said we are not to lay up treasures in heaven and not on earth, stated that we cannot serve God and mammon. These are hard issues in a wealthy society, even for well-meaning Christians."* The choice is hard, but it is a simple choice. Do we give our allegiance to God or do we give our allegiance to money? I have been thinking a lot about money lately. I pray that God would bless me with more, so I might be able to give more to His Kingdom. Ultimately, He knows what is best for me and will provide all I have need of.

EXCHANGE OF EXPECTATIONS

It was a nice Fall morning in New York City. Three of us from our church were there for a pastor's conference organized by David

Wilkerson's Times Square Church. It was a wonderful and encouraging time of teaching and renewal presented by their pastoral staff in Radio City Music Hall. Before the meetings started one morning, we stopped into a café for breakfast. We had bagels, cream cheese, and some coffee. I will never forget the expression on my friend's face when we received the bill. It was around thirty dollars and we didn't get much. Sometimes what we are used to is not what is reality. Certainly, the price in a Manhattan café was much different than the price in a small country diner. Our expectations can be formed by years of doing things a certain way. Maybe our traditions or upbringing have set in us a certain degree of expectations. Or maybe the struggles that we have had in life have created them as well. Jesus wants us to know when we have exchanged our life for His, all things really do become new. Yes, we will still have earthly ramifications from the decisions of our past, but by His Grace, tomorrow will be different. For me, the struggles of fear, control, and anger no longer dominate my life cycles. Now, I still struggle occasionally, but I quickly remember who I am in Christ, and it makes all the difference.

No longer the old man

When I look back on my previous condition and state of mind, I was so stuck. But now I want to grow old with no regrets. We make mistakes, but we repent of our wrongdoing, seek forgiveness, and move on. We have to lay our deadly doing down. Instead of constantly trying to seek the acceptance of God, we need to simply rest in the acceptance that is already there in Christ. The Lord has given us a great promise in Scripture. He tells us of a great inheritance that is ours in eternity with Him. We must come to see that our focus cannot be on material things but eternal. In the Old Testament, the Levites' inheritance was unlike that of the other tribes. Numbers 18:20 says, *"Then the LORD said to Aaron: "You shall have no inheritance in their land, nor shall you have any portion among them; I am your portion and your inheritance among the children of Israel."* When we come to see that Christ is ours, we then realize we are very wealthy people.

A GOOD EXCHANGE RATE?

A friend from church generously gave me an authentic page out of a Geneva Bible dating back to 1640. Robert had come up to me one day in church and asked me what were some of my favorite Bible verses. A couple weeks earlier, he had shown me a copy of a page out of an old Bible, and I told him I was impressed. Just a few weeks later, he came up to me again and handed me a beautiful folder he had made. In it was that page that is now framed and hanging in my living room. On that page is a particularly special passage out of Galatians. In this passage, it clearly states when we are living a life in Jesus, that we experience an exchange. Galatians 2:20 says, *"I have been crucified with Christ; it is no longer I who live, but Christ lives in me; and the life which I now live in the flesh I live by faith in the Son of God, who loved me and gave Himself for me."* This verse is what this chapter is all about. When I walk through the living room and see this page of the Bible, it is a constant reminder of how far I have come. I was recently telling a friend that I had published a book before, but then had it taken out of print. That book was written during a time in my life when I was caught up in my anger cycles. There were some good points in it, but the message was not conveyed in love. And when a message is not conveyed in love, the Bible says it is like a clanging cymbal … just a bunch of noise. It is my prayer that this book would be accepted with the love in which it is being written. I am thankful for the exchange that Jesus has made possible for each one of us. Will you also be thankful to Him today?

CHAPTER 20:

SOURCE OF LIFE

Jesus you have cracked the crusty shell
Saturate me with the living water well
To a place of prayer I have never known
The depths of Christ love I wholeheartedly own

The Living Water well

John 7:37-38 says, *"On the last day, that great day of the feast, Jesus stood and cried out, saying, "If anyone thirsts, let him come to Me and drink. He who believes in Me, as the Scripture has said, out of his heart will flow rivers of living water."*

Jesus declared if we drink of Him, we will thirst no more. What are you thirsting for in your life right now? Is there some feeling of void that you cannot shake or maybe a conviction that will not let you go? Or have you been trying to find peace and happiness in all kinds of places? In the Bible, the story of the Samaritan woman at the well describes a life-changing encounter with Jesus. Unbeknownst to her, there stood Jesus Himself. He would tell her that she was forgiven, but that she should go and sin no more. When we partake of the living water of Jesus, we will not desire a liberty to sin, but rather, will enjoy the life transformation that His life in us brings. We all have certain cracks in life and problems we have slipped into. But regardless of our past, Jesus invites us to drink of Life.

WATER FOR KENYA

Living water is necessary for our spiritual and physical survival. I had not been in Kenya too long when I met a young man named Ezekiel. Ezekiel worked as a gardener and groundskeeper for the mission board I was associated with. The counseling center where I worked was on a wonderful piece of property about ten miles west of Nairobi. The gardens on the grounds were absolutely stunning, largely in part, because of Ezekiel's keen skill and ability. We became good friends, and after a couple months, he invited me to visit his family at their upcountry home in Mwingi District in Central Kenya. Many of the people I met while in Kenya worked in Nairobi but maintained a family home in their home villages. They would send money home to support their family and relatives, and would visit every month or two. The drive to his village was about three hours over several highways and then another hour over very rough country roads. As we drove through the dry creeks and dry river beds, Ezekiel told me about the severe drought they had been having. As we passed over one dry river, we watched as young boys were digging several feet down trying to strike water.

They had small buckets and were working very hard for a minimal amount. That first visit was eye-opening for me and it starting a process by which we would eventually dig a well and set-up a solar panel pumping system. I was back in the States when the well pump testing was performed. Ezekiel said people carried buckets over a several-mile trek back and forth for a twenty-four hour period while the pumps were running. I had always heard of people lacking water, but now, it was closer to home. I had met these people and watched as they worked so hard, just to find what I had an abundance of. Funds were raised so the well project could be completed. Water is now being used for irrigation projects, helping to grow much needed food in this drought-stricken place. Water is necessary to survive. It is a fantastic opportunity we have to share the wonderful news of Jesus with people, but it is also important to share help to provide physical needs as well. I am thankful for Ezekiel and his devotion to help care for the people in his area. My life was once like those dry river beds. When people go without water for too long, they will die. I had been going without the life-giving water of Jesus for too long. But once I found a place of prayer in those early mornings, my life started to change.

THE START TO MY DAY

I had always had plenty of water for my physical needs but was always a bit short on the spiritual living water from my prayer time. Getting up early has always been hard for me. When I look at people that enjoy getting up at 5:00, I really admire them. But for some reason it is really difficult for me when the alarm goes off and I just want to lay there. There is something very special about getting up early and sitting in the quiet with Bible in hand while praying. There is nothing miraculous about it. But when we give God our first time in the morning, without all the daily distractions, the results are always good. When I started getting up early each day to pray, before entering all the distractions, my days were more productive and enjoyable. There is something special about getting a fresh start with God in the morning. So many sermons have been taught on prayer. So many books have been written on prayer. And we often talk to one another about prayer. But will we pray? For some reason that is much more difficult. There is a great quote by Hudson Taylor on this matter. Taylor said, *"A word about the morning watch may not be out of place here. There is no time so profitably spent as the early hour given to JESUS only. Do we give sufficient attention to this hour? If possible, it should be redeemed; nothing can make up for it."* I would agree with Taylor that the best and most profitable hour of the day is that first early one alone with God.

THE ETERNAL MINDSET

From Mauna Kea on the Big Island of Hawaii, the view of the night stars is one of the most spectacular, if not the best, in the world. Gazing up at the Universe from that location should make even the most skeptical person aware of the majesty of God. At nearly 14,000 feet above sea-level, and in a location and environment best suited for star-gazing, it leaves the observer amazed. Even as wonderful as this is, the Bible describes a time in the future when God will roll up the heavens and earth like a scroll. The Apostle Paul, writing to the Corinthian people, declared the temporary nature of this world and life we live in. 2 Corinthians 4:18 says, *"While we do not look at things which are seen, but at the things which are not seen. For the things which are seen are temporary, but the things which are not seen are eternal."* He told them instead, to focus on that which is eternal in the heavenlies. The idea may sound strange to us, because we have to maintain and conduct ourselves in this life. So what was Paul really getting at? I believe God is telling us to let the eternal things motivate our current activities. Through prayer, and the saturation of the Living Water of Jesus, our desires and motivations should be changed. They will change in a way that coincides with Paul's letter to the Corinthians. Just as spending time with the Lord in prayer should make us more humble, it should also cause us to think more on heavenly things.

MORE EDUCATION

It is as if our minds are like a crusty shell that water simply runs off of. When gardening, you have to break the crust of the soil to let it breath and let the water penetrate the surface. I suspect our minds are kind of like that. Occasionally, God has to break up our crusty shells so His message can sink in. On a flight from Dallas to Rome, I sat next to a history professor from the University of California. He was on his way to speak at a conference about how to deal with fundamentalist religious views. I am thankful to have sat next to some pretty interesting people during my travels. Is it just by chance that I sat next to him? I don't believe so! I like hearing people's stories and he was just as excited to tell me about the upcoming conference. During that flight, he told me about his time growing up in India and then living in England. He was an interesting man, but as smart as he was, he was still not convinced God's Word was the only true religious book. I shared my testimony with him and told him what I believed the Bible said about heaven. I described my walk with God and shared the complete salvation message. He listened politely, but I don't think he agreed. And although he didn't agree, I felt a Godly-love toward him, desiring that he would eventually come to know Jesus in a personal way. It is so nice when people can share their different views and still enjoy talking to one another. People always want to talk about peace and getting everyone together. I am all for that. But with that should always be the liberty to discuss our religious views without persecution. However, history shows otherwise. Over the centuries people of different religious views have been persecuted for their faith. Unfortunately, it is still happening today. But no matter what the consequences are, we still must choose to share the love of the Gospel.

There is a God, and I am not Him

Henry Cloud wrote, *"Appreciate the things that we cannot know for sure. That is to allow God to be God and us to be human. Give up the need to have certainty and rules for everything."* When I have the opportunity to speak to people in my office that are struggling with life issues, they often end up speaking of some aspect of life they cannot understand. I am always sure to point out the fact that I am not either. I am so thankful I have given up trying to understand everything and understand why people are doing what they are doing. Ultimately, we are all God's children, and He loves us more than we love ourselves. When we come to a surrendered place of prayer, we stop wanting to understand everything, and instead, we start appreciating more. When we find ourselves in a state of questioning, it is often some sort of selfishness. But, when we find ourselves in a state of appreciation, it is a reflection of God's goodness in us. Let us not fall into the trap of tying to understand everything God is doing. This is a dangerous path to travel down. Our human minds cannot wrap themselves around the majesty of God, so let's just trust He knows what He is doing.

WOULD YOU TAKE THIS ADVICE?

The place of prayer is a holy place. It is a place where we as individuals can go to be in the presence of God. When we are in the presence of God, He prepares us for the work He has for us. It is important we are working in a way that is motivated by Him and not a way that is trying to impress Him. It is an easy trap to fall into, thinking our busy religious activity will be pleasing to God. Hudson Taylor wrote, *"Our attention is here drawn to a danger which is pre-eminently one of this day: the intense activity of our times may lead to zeal in service, to the neglect of personal communion; but such neglect will not only lessen the value of the service, but tend to incapacitate us for the highest service."* In my life, even though I was doing some good things, I was still missing that which Taylor called the highest service. What higher service could we have than spending time in the presence of God? There isn't one. Because when we do that, the actions flowing from it, will have great and lasting eternal value.

INTO THE HOLY OF HOLIES

When I think of the Holy of Holies described in the Old Testament of the Bible, I think of the majesty and holiness of God. As we started our descent into Kraków, I looked out the window. Taken back by what I was seeing, in the midst of the beautiful Polish countryside, I realized I was looking at Auschwitz-Birkenau. Surprised to have looked out at the right time, I hurriedly grabbed my camera before we passed, and took a photo. On February 15, 1942, the first Jews were transported to Auschwitz. One and a half million would eventually be murdered on that site in one of the most terrible atrocities in history. While in Israel, I was privileged to have visited the Yad Vashem Memorial in Jerusalem, remembering those killed in the Holocaust. Let us pray for Jerusalem, Israel, and God's people.

Joel 3:1-2 says, *"For behold, in those days and at that time, when I bring back the captives of Judah and Jerusalem, I will also gather all nations, and bring them down to the Valley of Jehoshaphat; and I will enter into judgment with them there on account of My people, My heritage Israel, whom they have scattered among the nations; they have also divided up My land."* And verse 32 says, *"And it shall come to pass that whoever calls on the name of the LORD shall be saved. For in Mount Zion and in Jerusalem there shall be deliverance, As the Lord has said, among the remnant whom the Lord calls."*

In my living room, hangs a photo of a Jewish family playing on a Mediterranean beach in Caesarea, Israel. Their faces are not shown, but it shows a wonderful looking family enjoying the day together. When I took that photo, it was a reminder to me that God loves us and God keeps His promises. The Bible describes a time when God's people would come back into their land. The image captured that day stands as a testimony of God's faithfulness and goodness. God has also been faithful to me in my life. I didn't always get the punishment I deserved because He was gracious to me. I am so thankful he saved me out of my bondage and showed me a place of prayer I had never known before.

CHAPTER 21:

CENTRAL FOCUS

To laugh, love, and live is my desire
With Christ at the center bringing me higher
Fully entrusted to His Grace now
With the armor of God, set to the plow

KEEPING IT REAL

When we are fully entrusted to His grace, the process of being brought unto God will be worth it. Men and woman of faith have suffered greatly over the years. But, in many cases, those trials brought about great inspiration and a renewed zeal for God. John Bunyon, while spending a 12-year prison sentence for non-conformity to the religious system of the day, wrote, "*I went on like that for the space of two years crying out against people's sins and their fearful state because of them. Then the Lord came in upon my own soul with some steady peace and comfort through Christ; for He gave me many sweet revelations of His blessed grace through Him. For that reason, I altered my preaching (for I still preached what I saw and felt). Therefore, I then labored greatly to hold forth Jesus Christ in all His offices, relations, and benefits unto the world. And I labored also to expose, condemn, and remove those false supports and props upon which the world leans and by which they fall and perish. I also steadily ministered these things as long as the others."* What an amazing testimony by Bunyon. People like Bunyon are the real heroes!

WHERE ELSE WOULD I GO?

Have you ever had a sense of complete and total peace? I have always had a little discomfort in my body. My metabolism works very fast and it is hard for me to sit still for a long time. My body burns a lot of calories; even when trying to gain a few pounds, I seem to have trouble putting the weight on. If I spend time stretching in the mornings, I feel so much better. But if I don't, I can feel the tightness throughout most of the day. So when I have a sensation of total relaxation and peace in my body, I take notice. One of those moments comes to mind. I was sitting on Royal Jordanian Flight 508 headed to Amman from Cairo. The light breakfast was wonderful ... a crescent roll with butter and peach jam along with some orange juice and a cup of hot tea. We had just flown over the Sinai Peninsula and were heading around southern Israel. I can remember having a sense of total relaxation during that simple but fantastic breakfast. We are told in the Bible that when we are with the Lord Jesus in heaven, we will find ourselves in a place that our earthly minds cannot even imagine. We are also told that we will feel no sadness or pain. That is quite an amazing thought. When I feel a moment of total relaxation in my present body I take notice. So to think of what it might be like in the presence of God is rather spectacular. In our present earthly bodies, we are continually bombarded with other than beneficial thoughts, temptations, worries, doubts, and fears. It is a relentless attack on our peace and contentment. It is hard for us to imagine living an existence without those emotional pulls, but we know it is a reality for our future. When we are fully entrusted to God, we can at least get close to that complete peace that awaits us.

SIGNIFICANT THINGS

Dad and I were privileged enough to have seen Michael Schumacher, one of the greatest Formula One race car drivers of all time, win the US Grand Prix in Indianapolis. What a great weekend that was! Dad bought tickets and we camped on one of the lots directly across from the track. We pitched our tent that weekend and enjoyed the time together as we experienced the finest in all of motorsports. If you have witnessed a Formula One standing start, you will understand what exhilaration that brings. When twenty of the most technologically-advanced racecars are all positioned on the starting grid with their engines revving high, it sends chills down your back. The crowd that day was spectacular with people from many different countries waving flags and blowing horns. It was an experience I will never forget. The race with amazing, and when Schumacher was taking a victory lap, I snapped a photo of him triumphantly pumping his fist in the air. Sadly, years later, Schumacher would be injured while snow-skiing with his family. The head injury he suffered would result in him being in a coma for many years to follow. At the time of this writing, his family has not released his full medical condition, but he is believed to still be recovering. This man was on the top of his career and had everything in life. But in one moment everything changed, impacting him and his family in a very serious way. I can remember praying to God specifically about his life. My prayer was that God would heal him. I am not aware of anything concerning his spiritual condition. But I pray if he needs to make things right with God, the Lord would be merciful to him, giving him another opportunity at life. When our central focus is God, we will be concerned for people that possibly do not know Him. And when our focus is on God, we will be better prepared for those unexpected moments that always happen in life.

NOT A PART OF LIFE, HE IS YOUR LIFE

In a very convicting sermon by the late David Wilkerson, he talked about what constituted the true church of Jesus Christ. With Scripture he laid out several characteristics he believed should be evident in our lives as Christians. One of those characteristics will be Jesus being the center of everything we do. The Bible tells us to put on the whole armor of God so we might be protected and useful for His work. When Jesus is at the center of everything we do, we can trust our desires and motivations will be in line with His Word. It has been estimated that we are subjected to over 3000 advertising messages everyday. From commercials, billboards, internet ads, street signs, banners, flyers, mail, email, and the list goes on and on. Our minds are constantly being bombarded with messages from every conceivable source that wants to get our attention. And it doesn't stop with companies wanting to sell us things, but there is also a battle for our beliefs. No wonder we are a little tired. Maybe this is why it is so nice to simply take a walk in nature to get away from all the distractions.

But in a world with so many possibilities, how do we keep our focus? For the Christian that wants an intimate relationship with Jesus it can be hard. There is such a push to take God out of our institutions and our religious liberties are at risk. Even though the world may be against us, God is for us. That is not just religious talk. That is Scriptural. If we will take the time each day to spend time in prayer and in the Bible, God will carry us through. The Holy Spirit will help us decipher through all the messages to determine which ones are real. And when this it happening, we will want to focus on our heavenly treasure, instead of what the world has to offer. Matthew 6:19-21 says, *"Do not lay up for yourselves treasures on earth, where moth and rust destroy and where thieves break in and steal; but lay up for yourselves treasures in heaven, where neither moth nor rust destroys and where thieves do not break in and steal."*

THE ARMOR OF GOD

Chuck Missler said, *"We should not contaminate our hermeneutical hygiene with non-biblical nomenclature … because if you leave the authentic for synthetic, you're ripe for deception."* We need to let the Bible speak for itself, taking the literal meaning in black and white … well, and red. If we start trying to twist the Word of God to fit our agenda, we will start down a path of dilution. The Bible says that if one tries to add or delete anything from Scripture, let that man be accursed. That doesn't sound good to me. And the thought of trying to change Scripture to fit our agenda sounds a lot like trying to start a new religion. And Lord knows we do not need another religion. When we spend quality time in our Bibles and that time is covered in prayer, the Word of God takes root in us. As we get to know God more intimately in our prayer time, His Word coming into our life makes more sense. When one knows the author of something, they can better understand what the author is trying to say. If we truly want to know what God is saying, it is important to be able to confirm what we are hearing in prayer by what the Word of God says. There has been so much fallacy in the name of "God told me this" and "God told me that" … but does the Bible confirm these things should always be the question. We as humans are emotional people and our emotions can be very strong. We are all susceptible to making this type of mistake, myself included. This is why time in God's Word is so important. It is the defining text. You might hear a lot of people talking about what a commentary said about this verse or that verse. But, don't forget, the Bible is a commentary on the commentaries.

Consequences of versus Requirements for

When God set me free from the terrible bondage I had been in, I realized something about my actions. I used to look at my walk with God as a set of rules and do's and don'ts. But when the grace of God came into my life, those "requirements for" suddenly changed to "consequences of." All of the things that I had been trying to put into action to please God had failed. But when His grace became active in me, the consequences were the things I could never accomplish before…peace, contentment, and a deeper love for others. Are you still striving? Are you still trying to be a "human-doing?" Begin to let God work in you so you can be at rest. Become the "human-being" He intended for you to be.

WHAT DO YOU HAVE TO LOSE?

In a world of almost limitless options, what would you trade for Everything? As kids, we used to trade baseball cards at school. We liked it when the bus arrived at school a little early, so we would have time to talk before class started. As much fun as we did have, I probably gave away more than I gained. I have never been that good at trading things. And I don't know about you, but I am especially bad when it comes to trading automobiles. I guess I am just not that good of a negotiator. I am so glad I don't have to have negotiation skills when it comes to my walk with God. If you find yourself always trying to figure things out, there is hope aside from that. It is my hope, that for those reading through these pages, the words will inspire you to grow through whatever adversity you may be going through. When we come to see what the Lord has for us, we will be willing to give everything. What a fantastic trade for us as believers. We will all face challenges in our relationships. Some people will handle those challenges better than others, but there is still hope. When our central focus turns back to God, he can begin healing us. When I look back at the emotional trouble I had in my life and the pain I caused others, I only wish I would have made corrections sooner. But now, I have a wonderful relationship and feel complete in my daily walk with God. What used to seem impossible, has now become reality. Being able to enjoy the little things in life was a huge change for me that cannot be overstated.

Although my writing is not always the best, I have made an effort to put that gratitude into words. I am so thankful God loved me enough to help me through the struggles. If you are in a hurtful relationship, please know there is hope. There is hope for the healing possible through humility, faith, and love. And if you are like me, and the relationship ends, you can still look forward to joyful days ahead. Life is sometimes hard, but we must maintain a proper sense of reality. Being real in our daily life before God is absolutely vital to our success.

WHERE WILL HE TAKE ME TOMORROW?

As I sat under the pavilion overlooking the Pacific Ocean in Kona, Hawaii, two words came to mind. Confidence and kindness. It was March 24, 2019 at 2:15 on a beautiful afternoon. Yanching and I sat together drinking a wonderful cup of coffee in the midst of the lovely fountain pool under the surrounding palm trees. It really was a priceless view and a priceless experience. What amazing changes we experience in life. There were times when Yanching would be driving back home after giving people tours of various parts of the Big Island, Hawaii. She would often call and ask how I was doing. It was during those times, that we really became close and got to know each other. We would talk about different things in our lives and emotions we both faced. She found me to be a calming voice in her life and I was excited to be able to help. She actually did the same for me. After all that time of being alone, it was so nice to have someone to share my deepest feelings with. The Lord said, "It is not good for man to be alone." And I can attest to that. It is moments like these that are so special. I am very thankful for her.

For those of you having a hard time believing it will ever get better, believe me it does! Just keep trusting God, get up each day, take care of business, love people, brush your teeth, get some water, get some green vegetables, and keep going ... one breath, one step, one day at a time.

CHAPTER 22:

HUMBLE WALK

In an engulfing love there is no strife
Ministry to others will now be my life
An incredible thing happened to me
Lord, use this story to set captives free

EXCITED

Psalm 84:10 says, "*For a day in Your courts is better than a thousand. I would rather be a doorkeeper in the house of my God than dwell in the tents of wickedness.*" When I read a verse like this, it makes me excited. It is my opinion when we read this verse and it makes us smile inside, we can know we are on the right path. Are you excited today about the work God is doing in your life? Shouldn't we as Christians be excited about the life that Jesus has given us? And if you are not a Christian, could you be excited about the prospect of serving God by following His Son Jesus in the future? I pray you would be open to that. When I think about being excited, I think of people at a sporting event. It is interesting when we go to a baseball game and cheer for a guy hitting a homerun, people call us fans. But when we get up in church and get excited about the Creator of the Universe, people call us fanatics. Should we not be as much or more excited about Jesus as we are about a ballgame? I believe we should.

PEACE AMONG MEN

Even though my life is much different now, I must admit there are still times of sadness. I have been forgiven of my past mistakes, but the memories are still there. And there are consequences rendered that still must be faced each day. Sometimes the memories come back like an overwhelming flood. Just several days prior to writing this section, a flood like that came over me. It was a terrible flood of sadness, thinking about the emotional pain I had caused people in my past, and the emotional pain I had caused myself. The ripple effect of sin, even though that sin is forgiven, can have, and often will have, long lasting effects. When sin is winning the day, the pain that results from it does not only hurt ourselves and those around us, but it can have a generational impact as well. I pray that my six children would find complete forgiveness in their hearts for the trouble we had in our family. By doing so, I believe they will also have the freedom in Christ to be successful in theirs.

PRIDE BEFORE A FALL

The apostle Paul said he had a thorn in his flesh that kept him humble and surrendered before God. We are not told in Scripture what

Paul's issue was in his life, but maybe it is not important. I believe that really is the point. Paul's specific issue was not for us to know, because we all have something different to carry. The point is that it kept him in a state whereby he knew he needed God. God will not always take our afflictions away, but He will carry us through them. It is a place of humility. In my life, I had to be humiliated. That process of humiliation brought about humility. Andrew Murray said, *"The great test of whether the holiness we profess to seek or to attain, in truth and life, will be whether it be manifest in the increasing humility it produces."* What a remarkable statement by Murray. So now, in my life, I look to see whether or not I am becoming my humble or more prideful. The discovery upon that examination tells me a lot about my relationship with God. I pray I would increase in my humility so God can use me of service to Him.

AMAZED AT MY LIFE

I am thankful for my life. Up until this point, it has been a very interesting forty-eight years. I look forward to what will happen next. The thought occurred to me several weeks ago, that I have more adult life to live than adult life I have lived. Of course, this is Lord willing that He would give me another thirty or forty years. But at this stage of my life, I begin a new chapter in the wonderful story of God's miraculous Grace. By His Grace, I was set free. And by His Grace, He will keep me in the future. I am thankful now, but things did not quite turn out like I thought they would. It was a humbling point of self-realization, that I could come to accept the reality of where I was, several years after the separation. There was a point at which, no one could convince me of anything. I was determined I could work things out the way I thought they should be. It was a hopeful emotion that was just part of the process. Several months after the separation and the sale of our house, my daughter and son-in-law were gracious enough to take me in. It was a good time for me to get my mind clear and sort things out. They lived on some acreage on a country gravel road in beautiful eastern Missouri. I would often go running down the gravel roads that wound back and forth between the cattle fields and trees. On one stretch of the road there was a bridge crossing a creek. I would always stop on that bridge, pick up two rocks, and throw them into the wading pool below. I would watch as two ripples would form where the rocks penetrated the water. The two ripples would eventually meet each other in the center of the pool. After a few moments, those two ripple patterns would become one. It may sound crazy, but I envisioned the one rock being me and the other being my ex-wife. The two patterns would eventually fade into one, peaceful and gentle. At that time, early in the process, that was my thought and desire. About two years later, I realized the ripple patterns in our lives would never intersect like they did in that wading pool in the creek. It was a hard realization, but when the realization became clear, it was liberating. When you are going through something so difficult and then come to true peace, you will be amazed. If you are going through some struggle of your own right now, please be reminded that it will get better. Keep your sights on God and He will lift you up. You may not get things back like you thought, but He may have something even better that you could not have imagined before. God gave you life. Be amazed by it.

An incredible story to tell

As I was standing on top of Art Hill in Forest Park one morning, I enjoyed the view over the lake below. While looking over the fountains at the bottom of the hill, an old movie came to mind. I have tried and tried to find out what the movie is called, but have not been able to find it. So, if anyone reading this knows what movie I am talking about, please let me know! But in the movie, the main character is a runner and he is trying to qualify for the team. But because of his Jewish background, he is discriminated against. He wonders if he will ever be good enough and it bothers him that he is not accepted as an equal. The movie shows his efforts and eventually he is good enough to make it, but is still not accepted. One of the last scenes of the movie shows him running his race by himself with a stopwatch. When he crosses the finish line, he clicks the stopwatch, looks down at it, and realizes he has run the time he needed. No one is watching, only he is there and knows what he has done. With that satisfaction in his mind, and contentment on his face, he takes the watch and throws it away. The scene is powerful, because he came to the place where he knew he could do it, and was then content with himself. No one was there to witness it, but he walked away knowing he was good enough. In my life, I had to come to the place where I knew I was good enough. I knew that I was good enough before God, and didn't have to prove myself to anyone. I had spent a good part of my life trying to prove something to myself and others, but when I found peace in God, that was finally enough. I am so thankful for that realization.

WHAT IN THE WORLD ARE YOU DOING FOR GOD'S SAKE?

Let us be sympathetic to one another. One of my pastor friends asked a somewhat philosophical question after visiting Guatemala City. He asked, "What is worse … poverty or materialism?" Kind of a silly question really, but the fact is they both have their devastating extremes. With the prosperity that God can sometimes grant comes a huge responsibility in stewardship and humility. When we are in need, our tendency is to reach out to God for help. But when we have plenty, too often, we neglect our relationship with him. We need to be sympathetic to all people. Period. When we see people through the lenses of God's love, then we can walk humbly with them. It doesn't matter how much or how little we each have, we are all the same in God's eyes. When we see each other in humility, there will be no strife. This is freedom. One author posed the question, "What would you do today if all jobs were volunteer?" This is an interesting question that deserves some thought. Certainly, we all have to make a living to function, but if we could start doing what we were intended to do, what a wonderful thing that would be. As I think about the rest of my life, I ask myself, "What are you doing for God's sake?" This is not some rhetorical question, but one of great importance. Maybe as I sit here and write this, part of my purpose is being unfolded. I can only pray that something of value will be deposited into someone's life. Whomever may read this, may it be a blessing to them. I pray, Lord, use this story to set some captive free from the bondage they may be in. What a terrible thing to be in a place of bondage. But what an amazing thing to be set free.

TRULY THANKFUL

In my dream early in the morning of December 26, 2011, I was at a center that cared for children. I was in some role or position of responsibility. A man brought a child to me (they both looked as they were from Asia and maybe specifically, India). They were being secretive when the young girl was telling/asking about a special book – God's Word. At that point, I took a Bible in her own language and gave it to her. At the sight of it, she quickly snatched it out of my arms, hugged it tightly against her chest, and cried with excitement. I immediately broke into tears. I had thought, "How I have taken this for granted!" After these things happened - the man that brought her left.

I cannot say I fully understood the entire meaning of this dream, but I know it represented a person needing something of great value, and I was there to share it with them. We live in a world that is lost and hurting. People are looking for something of value, something they can depend on. You and I have the opportunity to be that conduit through which God can bring His hope and salvation. I pray you will join me in this endeavor.

CHOOSE FREEDOM

In the 25th chapter of Matthew, we find the parable of the wise and foolish virgins. The passage states, "*Then the kingdom of heaven shall be likened to ten virgins who took their lamps and went out to meet the bridegroom. Now five of them were wise, and five were foolish. Those who were foolish took their lamps and took no oil with them, but the wise took oil in their vessels with their lamps. But while the bridegroom was delayed, they all slumbered and slept. And at midnight a cry was heard, behold, the bridegroom is coming, go out to meet him! Then all those virgins arose and trimmed their lamps. And the foolish said to the wise, give us some of your oil, for our lamps are going out. But the wise answered, saying no lest there should not be enough for us and you; but go rather to those who sell, and buy for yourselves. And while they went to buy, the bridegroom came, and those who were ready went in with him to the wedding; and the door was shut. Afterward the other virgins came also, saying, Lord Lord open to us! But he answered and said, assuredly I say to you, I do not know you. Watch therefore, for you know neither of the day nor the hour in which the Son of Man is coming."*

Our time on this earth is limited. The time we have left to decide to follow Christ is limited. We are not promised another day, so please, Let's be ready!

Ephesians 3:17-19 says, *"that Christ may dwell in your hearts through faith; that you, being rooted and grounded in love, may be able to comprehend with all the saints what is the width and length and depth and height - to know the love of Christ which passes knowledge; that you may be filled with all the fullness of God."*

LET'S DO THIS TOGETHER

How precious life is. I can remember looking into my daughters' eyes moments after they were born. Years later, as I look back on those vivid moments, the miracle of life is clear. As I look into their eyes today, I can still see them lying in the delivery room staring up at me, waiting for someone to love them and care for them. I am thankful to have children as a gift from the Lord. The Lord created you and I and He is now looking down at us. He looks into our eyes and desires that our gaze would be returned upon Him. He looks lovingly at us, wanting to save us and care for us. We are all born into this world in sin. As we navigate life, the Lord whispers in our ear, and asks us to receive Him. We often reject Him and throw off the conviction to surrender, but He still loves us. Our rejection takes us down paths we shouldn't go, and our pride hurts others and ourselves. But still, He loves us. Then He puts us through difficulties and trials, still wanting our attention. And finally, sometimes after years of running and heartache, we finally surrender. All along, He has been there, and at some point in time, we accept the work He has accomplished for us. It is a refining process, and one that is worth the very Blood of Jesus. Job 23:10 says, *"But He knows the way that I take; when He has test me, I shall come forth as gold."*

CONCLUSION

HAVE YOU EVER FELT LIKE YOU WERE SHIPWRECKED? OR have you felt as if your ship was so battered by the storm that you would not survive? It takes time. But over time, with God healing us, we will experience a change in ourselves and people will notice. In the book Robinson Crusoe, we read of his troubles, but also of the character's pursuit to see a better day. At the four-year point into his struggle, we find these words, "*In the middle of this work I finished my fourth year in this place, and kept my anniversary with the same devotion, and with as much comfort as ever before; for, by a constant and serious devotion to the Word of God, and by the assistance of His grace, I gained a different knowledge from what I had before. I entertained different notions of things. I looked new upon the world as a thing remote, which I had nothing to do with, no expectation from, and, indeed, no desires about. In a word, I had nothing indeed to do with it, nor was ever likely to have; so I thought it looked, as we may*

perhaps look upon it hereafter, namely; as a place I had lived in, but was come out of it; and well might I say, as Father Abraham to Dives, "Between me and thee is a great gulf fixed." I am different now. In a spiritual sense, I spent years on a deserted island, wondering if I would ever find safe shores again. But I have now walked across that great gulf fixed on the bridge of Christ's Salvation. What a miraculous thing that is! Some people have recently told me, "Chris, you are so pleasant to be around now. You really seem to enjoy yourself." This is true and I am thankful for the changes God has worked in me.

While we walk through life in this present world, we are presented with a multitude of challenges and opportunities. Throughout our nation, we need to get back to righteousness. As it goes in our pulpits, so will our nation's health be. Alexis de Tocqueville wrote, *"I sought for the greatness and genius of America in her commodious harbors and her ample rivers – and it was not there ... in her fertile fields and boundless forests and it was not there ... in her rich mines and her vast world commerce – and it was not there ... in her democratic Congress and her matchless Constitution – and it was not there. Not until I went into the churches of America and heard her pulpits flame with righteousness did I understand the secret of her genius and power."*

Yes, it would be great if our pulpits flamed with righteousness, but we need to start with ourselves. Over the past several years, I have been concentrating on myself. No longer do I seek to figure others out, but now humbly ask God to make me the person He desires. Throughout the chapters in this book, I have sought to tell a story. It wasn't always easy to write, but I am thankful to have completed it. I am a walking testimony of God's Grace. It is a miraculous thing how God loves us and wants to save us. Unlike the character Crusoe, I was not shipwrecked on a deserted island, but I was shipwrecked in my emotional and spiritual condition. As I sat on that island trying to survive over the past four years, a lot has taken place. It has been my intention to write open and honest and I trust the words chosen have made a connection with you. I wrote another book about ten years ago, but it was during that time of my life when I had so much anger. It was written from an attitude that I was going to straighten people out. When I look back on it, I am glad I took it out of circulation. Writing a book this time was much different. Instead of trying to arrogantly straighten others out, I wanted to write about how God straightened me out. What a difference God's Grace has made in my life! I am thankful.

WORKS CITED

Biegeleisen, John. *Morning Dew*. St. Louis, MO: Eden Publishing House, 1948.

Bonhoeffer, Dietrich. *Discipleship*. Minneapolis, MN: Fortress Press, 2003.

Bunyan, John. P*ilgrims Progress Prayer Book*. Tyndale, 1986.

Card, Michael. *A Sacred Sorrow*. Colorado Springs, CO: NavPress, 2005.

Chambers, Oswald. *My Utmost for His Highest*. New York: Dodd, Mead & Company, 1963.

Cymbala, Jim. *Fresh Power*. Grand Rapids, MI: Zondervan Publishing House, 2001.

Defoe, Daniel. *Robinson Crusoe.* Accelerated Christian Education, 1989.

Dubose, Francis M. Classics of Christian Missions. Nashville, TN: Broadman, 1979.

Fitzpatrick, Elyse M. *Counsel from the Cross: Connecting Broken People to the Love of Christ.* Wheaton, IL: Crossway, 2009.

Gentry, Robert V. *Creation's Tiny Mystery.* Knoxville, TN: Earth Science Associates, 2003.

Goldsworthy, Graeme. *Preaching the Whole Bible as Christian Scripture.* Grand Rapids, MI: Eerdmans Publishing Co., 2000.

Guthrie, Stan. *Missions in the Third Millennium.* Waynesboro, GA: Paternoster Publishing, 2000.

Grubb, Norman P. *C.T. Studd Cricketeer & Pioneer.* Fort Washington, PA: Christian Literature Crusade, 1994.

Harvey, Dave. *When Sinners Say I Do.* Wapwallopen, PA: Shepherd Press, 2007.

Hazelbaker, Edward L. *John Bunyan: Grace Abounding to the Chief of Sinners.* Alachua, FL: Bridge Logos, 2014.

Hewitt, James S. *Illustrations Unlimited.* Wheaton, IL: Tyndale House Publishers, Inc., 1988.

Krauss, Harry, MD. *The Cure.* Wheaton, IL: Crossway Books, 2008.

Kuhn, Isobel. *Ascent to the Tribes: Pioneering in North Thailand.* London, England: Lutterworth, 1956.

Levy, David M. *The Tabernacle: Shadows of the Messiah.* Bellmawr, NJ: The Friends of Israel Gospel Ministry, Inc., 2005.

Marr, Ron. *A Christianity That Really Works.* Springdale, PA: Whitaker House, 1993.

McElrath, William N. *To Be the First: Adventures of Adoniram Judson, America's First Foreign Missionary.* Nashville, TN: Broadman Press, 1976

Muller, George. *The Autobiography of George Muller.* New Kensington, PA: Whitaker House, 1984.

Muller, George. *Release the Power of Prayer.* New Kensington, PA: Whitaker House, 2000.

Murray, Andrew. *An Exciting New Life.* New Kensington, PA: Whitaker House, 1982.

Murray, Andrew. *Humility & Absolute Surrender.* Peabody, MA: Hendrickson Publishers Inc., 2005.

Nee, Watchman. *The Normal Christian Life.* Wheaton, IL: Tyndale House Publishers Inc., 1977.

Olson, Bruce. *Bruchko.* Lake Mary, FL: Creation House, 1995.

Plummer, Robert L. *40 Questions About Interpreting the Bible.* Grand Rapids, MI: Kregel Publications, 2010.

Reeves, Michael. *Delighting in the Trinity*. Downers Grove, IL: IVP Academic, 2012.

Sorenson, Stephen W. comp. *The Best of Jonathan Edwards*. Colorado Springs, CO Cook Communications Ministries, 2006.

Stanford, Miles J. *None But the Hungry Heart, A Devotional Anthology*. Colorado Springs, CO: Self-published, 1987.

Sheldon, Charles M. *In His Steps*. Grand Rapids, MI: Revell, 1984.

Sparks, Austin T. *School of Christ*. Lindale, TX: Wilkerson Trust Publications, 2000.

Spurgeon, Charles H. *Finding Peace in Life's Storms*. New Kensington, PA: Whitaker House, 1997.

Stott, John R. *The Cross of Christ*. Downers Grove, IL: IVP, 2006.

Taylor, Howard, Howard Taylor and James Hudson Taylor. *Biography of James Hudson Taylor*. London: Hodder and Stoughton, 1973.

Taylor, Hudson. *Union and Communion*. London, England: 2012

Tozier, A.W. *The Pursuit of God*. Public Domain

Tripp, Tedd. *Shepherding a Child's Heart*. Wapwallopen, PA: Shepherd Press, 1995.

Trumbull, Charles. *The Life That Wins*. Fort Washington, PA: CLC Publications, 2003.

Walker, Jean, comp 1980. *Fool and Fanatic? Quotations from the Letters of C. T. Studd.* Gerards Cross, England: Worldwide Evangelization Crusade

Wiersbe, Warren. *Be Comforted.* Colorado Springs, CO: David C Cook, 2009.

Wilkerson, David. *Hallowed Be Thy Names.* Lindale, TX: David Wilkerson Publications, Inc., 2001.

Wurmbrand, Richard. *Tortured for Christ.* 4th ed. Middlebury, IN: Living Sacrifice Books, 1985.

Wurmbrand, Richard. *With God in Solitary Confinement.* Middlebury, IN: Christian Missions to the Communist World, Inc., 1969.

Yarnell, Malcolm. *The Formation of Christian Doctrine.* Nashville, TN: B&H Academic, 2007.